Overcoming Common Problems

The Complete Carer's Guide

BRIDGET McCALL

First published in Great Britain in 2007

Sheldon Press
36 Causton Street
London SW1P 4ST

The author and publisher have made every effort to ensure that the
external website and email addresses included in this book are correct and
up to date at the time of going to press. The author and publisher are not
responsible for the content, quality or continuing accessibility of the sites.

The publisher and author acknowledge with thanks permission to
reproduce extracts from the following:

Hugh Marriott, *The Selfish Pig's Guide to Caring*, Polperro Heritage Press,
copyright © 2003

Every effort has been made to acknowledge fully the sources of material
reproduced in this book. The publisher apologizes for any omissions that
may remain and, if notified, will ensure that full acknowledgements are
made in a subsequent edition.

British Library Cataloguing-in-Publication Data
A catalogue record for this book is available from the British Library

ISBN 978–0–85969–995–2

1 3 5 7 9 10 8 6 4 2

Typeset by Fakenham Photosetting Ltd, Fakenham, Norfolk
Printed in Great Britain by Ashford Colour Press

Contents

Acknowledgements		iv
Introduction		v
About the author		vi
1	What is a carer?	1
2	Sources of information and advice	8
3	Healthcare professionals	17
4	Community care	29
5	Finances	40
6	Employment and education for carers	47
7	Emotional, psychological and spiritual impact	52
8	Respite care and holidays	61
9	Caring for children	69
10	Caring at a distance	79
11	Young carers	86
12	Stopping caring	94
Conclusion		100
Useful addresses		105
Notes		116
Further reading		118
Index		119

Acknowledgements

I would particularly like to thank all the carers who contributed personal experiences to this book. I am extremely grateful to them for their willingness to share their stories and for giving up so much of their time to talk to me.

I'd also like to acknowledge the many published resources mentioned in the text, which I have used as references while writing this book. In particular those published by Carers UK, the Princess Royal Trust for Carers, Contact a Family and on the government's information website <www.direct.gov.uk>.

In addition, a big thank you to the following people who provided information, ideas, helped me set up interviews, commented on drafts or simply gave me much needed moral support: Rena Brewin, Paulo Mata and the staff of the Islington Princess Royal Trust Carers Centre, Frances Carroll, Barbara Cormie, Wendy Darch, May Darke, Pat Good, Harrow Mencap Carers Support Group, Rosie Hayward, Julie Henbury, Sasha Henriques, Linda and Brian Hill, Fiona Marshall, Chris McCall, Joe and Rosemary McCall, Sue Peckitt, Diana Pert, Jenny, Pam and Neil Russell, Abi Vernon, Liz Williams, Michael, Fiona and Thomas Youngman.

Introduction

If you provide practical and emotional support to a relative or friend who needs help because they are ill, aged or disabled, then you are a carer and this book is for you. It aims to provide you with a practical guide to the main issues that commonly affect carers and to highlight some useful resources.

Each person's experience of caring will be individual. There is no prescription for the best way to care; each carer has to find solutions that work best for him or her. How much your life is affected depends on many factors, including:

- the particular health problems the person you are caring for has;
- the type and extent of the help needed;
- your relationship with the person;
- your own health/circumstances;
- the support available to you – other family members and friends, services/support groups in your local area.

While I am not a carer, I spent many years working with carers as the information manager for a neurological charity. This book is largely based on the needs identified by carers I met during this time and through interviewing others for this book.

Time and time again carers have told me that talking to other carers or reading about their lives has helped more than anything else. This book therefore contains the stories and comments of several carers in the hope that you will find this helpful. Some of the ways that you can meet other carers, for instance through carers' groups run by Carers UK or the Princess Royal Trust for Carers, are also discussed.

Throughout the book I make reference to many published materials and organizations that can provide you with further information. Contact addresses are listed at the end of the book.

About the author

Bridget McCall worked for 17 years for the Parkinson's Disease Society providing information to people with Parkinson's disease and their carers. Now a freelance writer and editor, she is the author of *Living with Parkinson's Disease* (Sheldon Press, 2006) and has produced a wide variety of print, electronic and audio-visual information resources.

1

What is a carer?

This book has been written for 'informal carers' – i.e. people who look after or provide support, voluntarily and without payment, to someone, usually but not always a relative, who is ill, aged or disabled. However, it is important to note that the term is sometimes also used to describe 'professional carers' who provide paid support to people who require help with daily and personal tasks because of illness or disability. Where the word is used in this book, it generally refers to informal carers – apart from a few exceptions where the distinction is made clear.

According to Carers UK, one of the UK's leading carers' organizations, there are around six million carers in the UK today – 58 per cent women, 42 per cent men. Over one million of these care for more than one person. Over two million people become carers every year and by 2037 the number of carers may have increased to nine million.[1]

The form that caring takes will depend greatly on the nature of the illness or disability involved. For some carers, the person they care for is fairly independent and able. They don't have to provide anything more than the occasional helping hand with practical tasks, but may provide a lot of emotional and practical support.

Where a very disabling illness or condition is involved, the caring tasks can be considerable and these carers spend much of their time helping the person with all kinds of practical daily and personal activities, such as washing, dressing, cooking and administering medication.

Although many carers live with the person they care for, you can still be a carer if you don't. For instance, many people care for elderly parents at a distance, cleaning, cooking, shopping, organizing services and finances, filling in forms, dealing with crises, and giving emotional support.

Many carers desperately want to care for the person they love and, despite the challenges, it can be a very rewarding experience. However, it can also be an extremely hard life, especially if the carer feels he or she has no choice in the matter, feels isolated, is struggling to make ends meet, has little support or has health problems. If this is your situation, although I don't want to pretend that there are magic solutions, help is often available to ease some of the burden – if you know where and how to access it. I hope this book will help you identify resources that may help solve particular difficulties you are experiencing. Carers I spoke to say that sometimes just solving one issue can make a big difference to how they feel or cope.

Carers' needs

Research has identified several key points that are essential to the well-being of most carers. These include:

- ensuring the well-being of the person they are caring for;
- information and education – on the health condition in question, being a carer, practical aspects (such moving and handling) and the help available;
- services to help carers with caring that also allow them to have a life of their own and ensure that their own health and well-being are maintained – such as respite care services and financial benefits;
- a say in the provision of these services;
- opportunities to meet others in a similar position.

Public recognition of carers

Feelings about the term 'carer' vary enormously. Some people don't see themselves as a carer, or dislike the term, because they feel the support they provide is a part of the relationship (parent, child, relative, partner, friend) they have with the person they are caring for. Others like having a word that recognizes what they do, highlights how difficult and demanding caring can be, and helps them to separate the job of caring from the rest of the things that make up their relationship and their life.

Michael, who cares at a distance for his father aged 90, says, 'I think the term "carer" has a huge range of meanings. Many people I know who are carers do not use the term about themselves, and neither do I. They are husbands, wives, daughters, etc. who are doing the best they can for their loved one. However, over time, I have come to realize that, while I may not see myself as a carer, which to me sounds professional, somewhat impersonal and a distinct role from son, someone has to take on a rather more organized caring role in order for my father to get the best possible care he needs. Physical distance means I might not be the one giving the care, but I certainly have to be the one organizing it.

'One of the things I have learnt is that caring for someone becomes all-encompassing, forcing other jobs and roles to fade into the background. Often this leads to minor obstacles becoming major molehills – for example, when my father cared for my mother, all home maintenance was put on hold. In fact, delaying simple things like having a shower fitted meant years of struggling with baths after she had a hip operation. Being more "clear-headed" about priorities would have made life a lot easier. So gradually, I am recognizing that sometimes thinking of yourself as a carer as a separate role from others you have is quite useful. To care well does require you to think about what is required of that "job" in a more detached "professional" way.'

Whether you like the term or not, it has given carers a much-needed higher profile in the public arena in recent years and encouraged the development of specific services.

Official recognition

The importance of the carer's role is becoming increasingly recognized in the UK through Carers Acts that specifically address carers' needs. Since the Carers (Recognition and Services) Act 1995[2] was implemented, carers can also ask for their own needs to be taken into account when services are planned for the person they are caring for.

Under the subsequent Carers and Disabled Children Act 2000,[3] carers are also entitled to have an assessment in their own right, even if the person they care for refuses to be assessed himself or herself. Local authorities can now provide services to carers as well as the person being cared for.

A further Act, the Carers (Equal Opportunities) Act 2004[4] promotes greater opportunities for carers in employment, education and leisure.

In 1999, the government published *Caring About Carers: A national strategy for carers* to acknowledge the value of carers in the community and develop information, support and care services for them.[5] Particular emphasis is placed on providing support to help carers in employment and those who are young carers. A website for carers[6] has also been developed <www.carers.gov.uk> providing information and facts about carers as well as details of services and benefits available.

Many statutory bodies, such as primary care trusts and social service departments, are developing specific carers' services, such as carers' workers and centres.

There are dedicated carers' organizations, such as Carers UK and the Princess Royal Trust for Carers, to provide carers with information and support as well as campaign on their behalf.

In addition, many voluntary organizations for specific health conditions have recognized the needs of carers and family members. As well as providing services specifically for carers, they are often involved in campaigning and awareness-raising activities focused specifically on carers' issues. (See Chapter 2: Sources of information and advice.)

Personal experiences

Eva

Eva and her husband Robin have been caring for their daughter, Clare, for 20 years, since she was diagnosed at the age of ten with a rare, progressive, neurological condition called generalized torsion dystonia. This means that every muscle can go into involuntary spasm, and is like having cramp all over your body. At first, Clare's symptoms were mild, affecting one hand, which made feeding herself difficult. They didn't get dramatically worse for a long time, but by 14 she could no longer walk. Clare now needs help with all aspects of personal care, including continence care, administering of medication and communication.

'Disability isolates people,' Eva says. 'When she was an adolescent I spent more time with her than you would normally spend with the average teenage girl. So going away to college when she was 16 was the best thing that ever happened to her. This was a specialist college for disabled people and despite what they say about mainstream facilities, a positive aspect of this was that for once she was not the one sticking out like a sore thumb – it was almost as if they were saying, "Well that goes without saying so we can forget it and get on with being at college".'

Although Clare now lives independently in her own bungalow about 15 minutes' drive from her parents, their caring role continues and includes helping her to recruit the professional carers who provide her with 24-hour care. When she was in hospital recently, they visited every day – partly to ensure that her particular needs were recognized and met.

Eva has considerable experience of health and social services as well as voluntary organizations because she worked as a volunteer advisor for the disability information network, DIAL. She is involved with a number of local initiatives, and is the carer representative for the local carers' network. She says, 'I feel passionately that for every one like me who knows how to fight, even if they don't want to, there are hundreds who don't. The least I can do is try to help them, and hopefully I make a difference. However, it's not just that; it also gives me a different interest – an intellectual exercise where I am Eva, not Robin's wife or Clare's mother. I need that.'

The suggestions she would make to other carers are:

- Make sure the disabled person has a proper and comprehensive care assessment that is reviewed every year.
- Insist on a carer's assessment and have a review each time the person you are caring for has one.
- Make sure you get a copy of any care plans drawn up and that your signature is on it.
- Get a benefit check, preferably from a non-government organization such as Citizens Advice.
- Know exactly what health and social care services should be providing so that you know what to fight for.
- Every time you speak to service providers, particularly on the telephone, who agree to do something for you, send an email or letter afterwards confirming the content of the conversation and what was agreed. This ensures that you have something in writing and gives you a stronger position to argue from if you need to.

Wendy

Wendy's father, who died about nine years ago, had Parkinson's disease and she spent many years helping her mother to care for him.

When Wendy was pregnant with her first child, she accompanied her father to the appointment where he was given his Parkinson's diagnosis. She was not surprised by the news, unlike her father, and was pleased to know what he had so she could investigate what they were dealing with. 'Although I knew a little about Parkinson's because I was a nurse, I didn't know anyone with the condition and the support provided was minimal. The consultant simply said, "I think you have Parkinson's. There is nothing I can do for you and you will get progressively worse. Go back to your GP when you are in trouble." It was the first time I had seen my father cry.'

Looking back, she feels she would have liked to have been given some time to discuss what Parkinson's was and a further appointment to ask questions once her father had got over the shock. Neither she nor her father were interested in treatment options at that stage; they just wanted someone to tell them what the disorder was, how it would develop, the problems they might meet and what would be available to help.

Over time, Wendy's life changed as a result of her father having Parkinson's, but not immediately. Her father's Parkinson's wasn't impinging too much on his life at that point, so emotional support was all she initially had to provide. The main thing she did was to try to find out more about the condition – something that was more difficult in the days before the Internet.

However, as her father's Parkinson's progressed it became apparent to her that her mother, although incredibly supportive and loving, needed support with the caring. So Wendy often took on care of him for a day to give her mother a break. They always ensured that her father was included in anything they did as a family, no matter how disabled he became. Wendy says, 'It is exhausting to think what my mother and I used to do and how we used to deal with situations that could be sometimes horrendous, but we did. I loved my dad and I was determined he was not going to be left out, ignored or treated like an alien because he had Parkinson's.'

Wendy had a busy life in addition to her caring responsibilities – she returned to work, had another baby and completed a degree course. Eventually, however, she had to give up work to care for her father. She says, 'Caring put a lot of pressure on my time. Any spare time was spent supporting him or mum, who was just amazing in the way she cared for him. No one could have cared more than she did. My tasks included helping with daily living activities such as dressing, washing, cooking and driving mum and dad to appointments. This meant I had less time with my family although my husband and daughters were fantastic in their support. Giving up work impacted on our finances and with two young children, things were not always easy. I still feel guilty sometimes that I didn't do enough or fight enough for services and that I sometimes hated having to give up a precious weekend to care for him.

'I spent a lot of time trying to organize support systems to help my father, such as a downstairs bathroom. We felt we were always having to fight to get support from the statutory and voluntary services and often became frustrated at the response.'

To other carers, Wendy says:

- Don't be afraid to find out all you can about the condition the person you are caring for has, and seek help from whoever can give it to you.
- Make contact with a local support or carers group, even if all you want is to receive their newsletter.

- Don't be afraid to ask questions of health and social care professionals – it often helps to make a list.
- Decide what you would like to happen and don't be afraid to voice it. Sadly, it is probably not possible to provide everything you want or need, but you can get advice about what is available.
- Always include the person you are caring for in any decisions that are made, and avoid taking over his or her life.
- Remember there is a life outside caring and do as much as you can even if you have to coordinate other people to achieve it. Most people are only too willing to help.
- Above all be kind to yourself and remember that we are all human.

2

Sources of information and advice

Two factors hold the key to surviving as a carer – information and services. Carers generally need two types:

- to help them care for the person they are caring for;
- to support them as a carer.

Sometimes carers are lucky. Healthcare professionals give them lots of help and advice and/or put them in contact with services and organizations that can help.

For others, finding the right help can be an uphill struggle. Many feel confused about the role of the various healthcare professionals, or find that the advice one discipline gives them conflicts with that provided by another. One carer said, 'It seems to be a mysterious world of quangos, societies, self-help groups.'

There can also be a distinct lack of communication between different services so that carers find themselves endlessly repeating the same details over and over again. I am an information professional with many years' experience of working for a charity, yet there have been times while writing this book when locating even the most basic information on services I know exist has been a fruitless task. It must at times seem an impossible task for carers who are starting from scratch! One carer with experience of working for a voluntary organization said, 'It's not about them knowing everything but just the right places to signpost carers to.'

I cannot pretend there is an easy solution. Unfortunately the secret is often to persevere and to be insistent – something a tired, stressed carer can find extremely difficult and frustrating. Hopefully, the government's national carers' strategy, recent legislation, and the work of carers' organizations are gradually improving this. The moves to develop electronic patient records may also help in time. This chapter on finding information and advice resources, and the next two on healthcare professionals and community care are intended to help you in your search.

Carers' organizations

There are two main carers' organizations in the UK – Carers UK and the Princess Royal Trust for Carers, which provide invaluable support to carers.

Carers UK

Carers UK is a voluntary organization set up in 1965 to give carers a voice and to fight for the recognition and support that carers need and deserve. It aims to:

- transform the understanding of caring so that carers are free from discrimination and are valued by society;
- mobilize carers, decision-makers and the public to bring about the changes that make a real difference to carers' lives;
- inform carers of their rights, what help is available and how to challenge injustice so they can lead fulfilled lives.

Carers UK has been set up and led by carers. It provides information to carers about their rights and available help so they can make informed choices about their lives. This includes:

- a free advice service, CarersLine, which receives around 50,000 enquiries a year;
- *Caring* – a lively and informative magazine about carers' lives;
- a comprehensive website full of information on all aspects of caring <www.carersuk.org.uk>;
- a network of over 600 branches and affiliates providing support to carers on a local level.

Campaigning for a better deal for carers is a crucial part of their work. Carers UK has been at the forefront of securing legal rights for carers, including important legislation such as the Carers (Recognition and Services) Act 1995, the Carers and Disabled Children Act 2000, which gave carers certain rights such as assessments of their own needs as well as the person they are caring for and, most recently, the Carers (Equal Opportunities) Act 2004, which tackles the barriers carers face in accessing employment, education and leisure.

Carers UK is also the lead partner on Action for Carers and Employment (ACE), a project part-funded by the European Social Fund's Equal programme. This aims to raise awareness of the barriers facing carers who want to work, and to test and promote ways of supporting them (see Chapter 6: Employment and education for carers).

Many carers also face poverty as a result of their caring responsibility and Carers UK have tackled this through their Fair Deal Campaign, which resulted in a rise in carers' benefits, improvements in the pension provision for carers, and carers over the age of 65 being able to claim Carer's Allowance.

Recognition for carers within the health services has also been a priority. Their work has resulted in the new GP contract providing a financial incentive to the primary care team to identify and support carers and new guidance being issued to hospitals on how carers should be involved in decision-making about care of a patient when they are being discharged from hospital.

Training and advice for professionals who work with carers is also an important part of Carers UK's work.

The Princess Royal Trust for Carers

The Princess Royal Trust for Carers was set up in 1991 as an initiative of Her Royal Highness The Princess Royal. Through its 118 carers' centres, young carers' services and interactive website, the Trust provides information, advice and support services to carers.

Carers reading this book are most likely to have contact with one of the Trust's carers' centres. Each one is independently managed and their size and operation vary considerably, depending on local need and existing services. In a rural area, transport may be a primary concern, whereas in an urban area, a centre's work may concentrate more on working with other services. In an area with a diverse population, translating materials into key community languages may be a priority.

To give you some idea of the kind of services that a carers' centre might provide, I talked to Rena Brewin, who is a development worker at Islington Carers Forum, London, one of the larger Princess Royal Trust for Carers centres, which aims to support local people looking after ill or disabled friends and relatives.

As well as providing information and support, it also provides support to former carers, particularly immediately after they have stopped caring, perhaps because the person they were caring for has died, is at a residential school or now lives in a care home.

Also important is helping people to apply for benefits, signposting people to sources of help about housing issues and encouraging people to apply for community care assessments. The centre also helps with related mental health and drug or alcohol problems.

Meetings for carers usually include speakers on subjects of interest, such as new legislation; there are also regular outings and 'relaxing days' where carers can take advantage of a variety of complementary therapies.

Among Rena's most successful initiatives have been 'Back to Work' courses. As well as goal-planning, the courses focus on building confidence, raising self-esteem, identifying strengths, and developing assertiveness, stress and time-management skills. Carers are encouraged to recognize their skills and how to match these and their interests to possible job opportunities. They then move on to job-seeking skills, such as CVs, applications and interviews. At the last session, local employment and educational establishments are encouraged to attend to promote their services.

Rena says, 'I always emphasize the positive aspects of caring, and encourage carers to see that it is a job that people do value, and that they do have an identity as a carer. Not everyone does eventually go on to work but practically everyone goes on to do some kind of further education course. Some carers use the course to identify part-time work opportunities they can fit round their caring responsibilities. Others realize that employment isn't possible for them at present but they can still do positive things to help themselves meantime, such as keeping up their computer skills.'

Flexible respite care is another scheme. As well as funding more traditional types of respite care, the centre may also help with other breaks such as driving lessons, a gym subscription, a course of complementary therapy, college courses and home gym equipment.

This is just an example of how a local centre may work, and different centres do vary. To find your local carers centre, see the Trust's website or contact their national office.

Other carers' workers and centres

Many local councils and primary care trusts are also developing services, centres and workers specifically for carers. Your local social services department, GP surgery or Citizens Advice should be able to advise you on what is available in your area.

Black and minority ethnic carers

According to a policy briefing published in 1998 by Carers UK, there may be as many 285,000 black and minority ethnic carers in the UK.[7] This group of carers may face additional barriers to obtaining information and services to meet their needs. These may include communication difficulties such as language barriers and a dearth of resources in their community languages, difficulties in accessing services, lack of culturally appropriate and responsive services. The concept of 'carer' may not exist in some communities. Cultural attitudes towards disability vary and in some cases can alienate the carer.[8]

Carers UK and the Princess Royal Trust for Carers can advise further on black and minority carer issues. Many voluntary organizations may also help. For example, Mencap has developed some local services specifically for black and minority ethnic communities.

Gay and lesbian carers

According to Carers UK, there may be 300,000 or more gay and lesbian carers in the UK.[9] Their policy briefing published in 2003 highlights the fact that many experience additional obstacles in accessing support and services through prejudice and lack of legal recognition. This may include homophobia, isolation, having to 'come out', non-recognition by professionals and financial issues. Hopefully the civil partnership registration scheme will help overcome some of these barriers.

Carers UK and the Princess Royal Trust for Carers should be able to advise further. Some voluntary organizations have developed services specifically for gay and lesbian carers. For example, the Alzheimer's Society has a gay and lesbian network, including a telephone helpline that is staffed by gay men and lesbian women, and a dedicated web page. Age Concern is developing a series of publications for gay, lesbian and bisexual people through its Opening Doors project <www.ageconcern.org.uk/openingdoors>.

Voluntary organizations

Obtaining information about the health condition you are dealing with can make your life as a carer easier and ensure that you and the person you are caring for can make informed choices about care.

The UK has an enormous number of voluntary organizations that cater for a very broad range of need and interests. They usually operate independently from government or business on a self-governing, self-funding (through donations and fundraising initiatives) and not-for-profit basis. Although many have paid staff, they often rely heavily on volunteers to help them run their activities. Some examples are:

• cancer – Macmillan Cancer Support, Cancerbackup;

- learning disability – Mencap (Enable in Scotland), Foundation for People with Learning Difficulties, the Down's Syndrome Association, the National Autistic Society, Mind;
- long-term illnesses – Arthritis Care, the Brain & Spine Foundation, British Heart Foundation, the Stroke Association, Diabetes UK, the MS Society, the Motor Neurone Association, Parkinson's Disease Society;
- mental health – the Depression Alliance, MDF The BiPolar Organisation, Mental Health Foundation, Mind, the Scottish Association for Mental Health, the Northern Ireland Association for Mental Health, Rethink, Samaritans, Sane;
- dementia – the Alzheimer's Society, Alzheimer Scotland – Action on Dementia.

Those that focus on health and social care issues or aspects of living with a chronic illness or disability are also likely to be of interest. These include those concerned with:

- ageing – Age Concern, Help the Aged, Action on Elder Abuse, Counsel and Care;
- disability issues – Royal Association for Disability and Rehabilitation (RADAR);
- children – Barnardo's, the Children's Society, Contact a Family, NCH, the children's charity;
- terminal/life-limiting conditions – Help the Hospices.

The first step is to find out if there is a voluntary organization or charity that supports people with the health condition you are dealing with. As well as providing resources, such as leaflets, booklets, websites, regular newsletters, helplines and local support groups, these often have specific services for carers.

The National Council for Voluntary Organizations publishes the Voluntary Agencies Directory, an annual reference guide to over 2000 national charities and organizations connected to the voluntary sector. Your local reference library should have copies of this and other books that provide details of voluntary organizations in the UK such as Charity Choice/Charities Digest (see online version at <www.charity-choice.co.uk>).

Patient UK is a useful online resource produced by two GPs. This evidence-based website provides a wealth of information on health conditions, maintaining a healthy lifestyle and contact details for many voluntary organizations. See <www.patient.co.uk>.

Citizens Advice is a major source of information and advice that you will find mentioned several times in this book. It helps people resolve their legal, financial and other problems, providing free information and advice and signposting other sources of help. It provides independent advice from over 3,000 locations including bureaux, GP surgeries, hospitals, colleges, prisons and courts. It also has an Internet advice guide, which includes frequently asked questions in a number of community languages – see <www.adviceguide.org.uk>. The number of your local bureau should be in the phone directory, or available from your library or the Citizens Advice website – see <www.citizensadvice.org.uk>.

Rare disorders

There are more than 5,000 known rare disorders that affect children and adults[10] and probably many more that have not yet been identified. Finding information on diagnosis, treatment and care on these conditions can be very difficult and caring for someone with a rare disorder can be a very isolating, lonely experience. The following organizations support people with rare disorders and their families and campaign on issues affecting people who have these conditions.

Contact a Family, a charity that helps families with disabled children, provides information and support to anyone affected by a rare disorder and publishes a directory of specific conditions and rare disorders. It also tries to put people in touch with others in a similar situation through its family linking scheme.

Contact a Family also publishes a fact sheet, 'Living without a Diagnosis', because many families never receive a definite diagnosis and the needs of these families can be similar to those affected by a rare condition.

Eurodis is a European organization for rare disorders that represents more than 260 rare disease organizations (covering over 1,000 rare diseases) in over 30 countries. Its website provides a guide to finding information on rare disorders and links to many sources of help.

Orphanet <www.orpha.net> is a European database of rare diseases and orphan drugs (i.e. medications used by a small number of people).

Medical information and the media

Developments in information technology, such as the Internet, have made huge volumes of material available to anyone with access to a computer. Sifting through it all can be overwhelming and confusing.

Although there are some excellent sites, there are also many that contain very inaccurate or dubious material. How do you ascertain what is useful, validated information and what is not?

Concerns about the credibility of information is particularly pertinent with respect to complementary therapies, an interesting area of health with many genuine practitioners but one which also attracts a lot of people peddling all sorts of 'miracle cures'. Many of these are marketed in a way that makes them seem more credible than they are, often making claims that 'research has proved their efficacy'. Even if this is true, there are different levels of research and sometimes the 'proof' is based on very flimsy or questionable standards – even when they provide lots of references.

Bandolier is an independent journal and website about evidence-based healthcare written by Oxford scientists. On its website, they say that 'the impetus behind Bandolier was to find information about evidence of effectiveness (or lack of it), and put the results forward as simple bullet points of those that worked and those that did not: a bandolier with bullets'. See <www.jr2.ox.ac.uk/bandolier>.

Quackwatch is a non-profit organization, set up by a retired doctor, which is based in the USA but has an international focus in attempting to 'combat health-related frauds, myths, fads, and fallacies'. See <www.quackwatch.org>.

The British Medical Association (BMA) publishes a guide to 'Finding reliable health information on the internet' on its website (<www.bma.org.uk>). The *British Medical Journal* (BMJ) has also recently launched a website called 'Best Treatments' that aims to provide evidence-based information to lay people – see <www.best-treatments.co.uk>.

Contact a Family has a good article, 'Medical Information on the Internet: Seeking Quality', on its website. See <www.cafamily.org.uk>.

General sources of information

Age Concern produces carers' handbooks that provide information on decisions that need to be taken, options available, practical checklists and case studies, and specialist help from health and social services. These include caring in general, and caring for people with particular conditions or situations, including alcohol problems, arthritis, at a distance, cancer, diabetes, hearing loss, heart, memory loss, stroke and people who are dying.

The BBC website <www.bbc.co.uk> has a wealth of information on health, relationships, caring and parenting, including personal stories, which many carers will find helpful.

Sheldon Press, the publisher of this book, publishes a wide range of concise, practical health and self-help guides. See <www.sheldonpress. co.uk> for more information.

Your local library

Your local library should be able to help you access information. It may stock the published resources or you can ask it to purchase or borrow them from another library. Libraries also offer many other services, including reference books, contact details for local services and organizations, Internet access, information/enquiry services, education courses and photocopying facilities. They often also provide services to people who are housebound.

Personal experiences

Wendy says, 'My mother and I found going to the local Parkinson's Disease Society branch meetings very helpful because we realized that we were not alone, and gained a lot from the mutual support they provided. We made many friends and I liked the fact that we often talked about other things than Parkinson's, because it can so take over your life. There was always lots of laughter at the meetings.'

3

Healthcare professionals

This chapter provides an overview of the main types of healthcare professionals that you may come across. Hopefully this will throw a little light on an often complex system, and help clarify what the different professionals may be able to provide, and how you access them. Your local Patient and Liaison Service (described later in this chapter) or carers centre (see Chapter 2: Sources of information and advice) should be able to advise further.

NHS Direct and NHS24

The National Health Service (NHS) has a 24-hour nurse-led telephone information service on health services or conditions, NHS Direct – 0845 4647. In Scotland, there is a similar service, NHS24 – 08454 242424.

The NHS Direct websites are also useful resources for information on health conditions and issues, and the other websites listed here provide more information on how the NHS works:

England and Northern Ireland – www.nhsdirect.co.uk
Wales – www.nhsdirect.wales.nhs.uk
Scotland – www.nhs24.co.uk
England – www.nhs.uk
Northern Ireland – www.healthandcareni.co.uk
Scotland – www.show.scot.nhs.uk
Wales – www.wales.nhs.uk
Isle of Man – www.gov.im/dhss.health/
Guernsey – www.gov.gg/ccm/navigation/health_social-services/
Jersey – www.gov.je/HealthWell

Primary care

The Department of Health describes primary care as 'the health services that play a central role in the local community, such as family doctors (GPs), pharmacists, dentists and midwives'.[11]

These are managed by primary care trusts. Services they cover include:

- GPs
- hospitals
- dentists
- opticians
- pharmacies
- mental health services
- walk-in centres
- patient transport (including accident and emergency services)
- population screening.

Patient Advice and Liaison Services (PALS)

All primary care trusts have Patient Advice and Liaison Services (PALS). These aim to:

- provide you with help and information on local healthcare services and support agencies;
- offer practical advice to help resolve difficulties that you may have when using any NHS services or if you don't know how to access them;
- give you a say in your own care and how your local services operate.

They also provide information to the primary care trust board about concerns that patients have expressed about services so that problems can be solved and services improved. They cannot get involved in formal complaints but can advise you about the NHS complaints system, including local Independent Complaint Advocacy Services (ICAS), which can support people making a formal complaint.

Your local primary care trust, GP surgery or hospital should be able to provide you with contact details for your local PALS.

Secondary care

Secondary care involves hospital healthcare. Secondary care services may involve:

- an outpatient appointment to see a consultant or other healthcare professional;

- day services, such as tests, minor surgery and rehabilitation services in day hospital settings;
- inpatient treatment for diagnosis, tests or treatment;
- emergency care.

Doctors

General Practitioners (GPs)

GPs are the first point of contact for most other medical services and will be a central resource to you, providing treatment, health advice and helping you to access the services you need. Some GP surgeries keep a register of carers or provide specific carer services, so it is worth asking what yours offers.

Many carers find it helpful to see a different GP for their own health needs, rather than the GP who looks after the person they are caring for. This can make it easier for them to discuss any problems they have as a carer without feeling that the GP may have a conflict of interest by treating both of them.

Hospital doctors

Many specialists work in multidisciplinary teams made up of a wide variety of healthcare professionals. They will also work with 'junior doctors' of varying ranks including senior registrar, registrar and foundation doctors. At some visits you may see these doctors rather than the consultant who leads the team.

Nurses

You may have contact with many nursing disciplines during your life as a carer.

Specialist nurses

In the UK, there are now specialist nurses for many conditions, e.g. cancer, diabetes, heart conditions, multiple sclerosis and Parkinson's disease. Nurse specialists may not be available in every area. Your GP surgery, PALS service or a voluntary organization dealing with the health condition in question should be able to advise you further.

Community nurses[12]

Carers may come into contact with several types of community nurses, who will usually be attached to a GP surgery or employed by a primary care trust. These include:

- *Practice nurses* are involved in many aspects of patient care and treatment within a GP surgery, including treating small injuries and assisting with minor operations, screening, family planning, vaccination and health promotion schemes.
- *District nurses* work in a variety of settings including GP surgeries, people's homes and residential homes. The aim of their work is to respond quickly and intensively to patients' needs to enable them to avoid hospital admission or be discharged early. Many of their patients will be elderly, recently discharged from hospital, disabled or terminally ill. Their role may include assessing and planning management of a patient; administration of drugs (including injections), blood transfusions and drips; health checks; and cleaning and dressing wounds.
- *Health visitors* focus on health promotion and prevention. They may advise mothers of young babies on childcare and health or help people with chronic illness or disability to overcome problems.
- *Mental health or psychiatric nurses* provide support to people of all ages who have mental health problems. They will often be responsible for coordinating a person's care in the community and liaising with other services that are involved.
- *Learning disability nurses* help people with a learning disability to maintain and improve their lifestyles and participate fully as equal members of society. This might include helping them to develop manual and recognition skills, find employment or bring up a family.

Dentists[13]

Going to the dentist can present a problem for some people who are ill or have disabilities. Primary care trusts (in England) and health boards (Scotland, Wales and Northern Ireland) run community dental services (sometimes known as salaried primary care dental services) to provide dental care for people who have difficulty getting treatment from general dental services. The dentists employed in this service may work in a variety of places including a person's home and care homes.

Contact your local primary care trust or health board for more information.

Opticians

Anyone who is eligible for an NHS sight test and is immobile should have access to a sight test and optical services that are provided in their own home (domiciliary eye care). For more information, contact your local primary care trust. The Eye Care Trust can provide information on all aspects of eye care.

Allied health professionals

Professions such as physiotherapy, speech and language therapy, occupational therapy, podiatry, and dietetics are often grouped together under the umbrella term 'allied health professionals'.

Physiotherapists

Physiotherapists deal with physical problems that occur as a result of injury, illness or ageing. Treatment may include exercise, heat treatments, manipulation, or hydrotherapy. Some of the ways they may help include:

- teaching techniques that help to make many everyday activities and movements that are affected by the illness or disability the person has easier to manage – including walking, sitting down, standing up;
- helping someone to maintain as much independence as possible;
- working on muscles and joints;
- falls prevention and management;
- pain relief;
- maintaining and improving effective breathing;
- management of circulatory problems that arise as a result of restricted mobility.

Physiotherapists can also advise carers, particularly on safe lifting and handling techniques that prevent injury to your own body (especially your back) and at the same time avoid harm to the person you are caring for.

Physiotherapists work in both hospital and community settings. To see an NHS physiotherapist you usually need a referral from your GP, specialist or Parkinson's disease nurse specialist. In some places you can refer yourself at the local hospital or community health clinic.

You can also see them privately. If you want to consider this option, you need to make sure that the physiotherapist you see is properly trained and specializes in the health condition in question. They will have MCSP (Member of the Charted Society of Physiotherapy) after their name. Contact the Chartered Society of Physiotherapists for more information.

Speech and language therapists

As well as treating speech, language and communication problems, speech and language therapists also help people with eating or swallowing problems.

Their role includes:

- providing exercises to improve communication that you can do on a one-to-one basis or in a group;
- suggesting breathing and postural techniques that can facilitate better communication;
- helping to make particular daily activities easier to manage – such as talking on the telephone;
- advising on suitable equipment to help with communication, swallowing, eating and drinking.

If you are a carer, you can also obtain advice on managing these problems from a speech and language therapist.

Speech and language therapists work in hospital and community settings. Referral is often via your GP, doctor or Parkinson's disease nurse specialist, although in many places you can refer yourself to an NHS speech and language therapist via your local hospital or health centre.

Some speech and language therapists also work in private practice. You need to ensure that any therapist you see is properly qualified – they will have the letters MRCSLT (Member of the Royal College of Speech and Language Therapists) after their name – and that they specialize in the health condition the person you are caring for has. Contact the Royal College of Speech and Language Therapists for more information.

Occupational therapists

Occupational therapists are trained to help people who have disabilities to remain as independent as possible and have a good quality of life. They tend to focus on individual needs, so the methods they employ will depend on the person's particular difficulties. Their advice might include:

- assessing activities that a person finds difficult and suggesting ways to make them easier – examples include washing, dressing, cooking, turning over in bed, housework;
- advising how to make home and work environments safer and easier to cope with – this might mean simply rearranging the furniture or it might include adaptations ranging from grab rails on stairs to walk-in showers in the bathroom;
- identifying equipment or technology to help you with particular tasks that you want to achieve;
- finding ways to make work or leisure activities easier;
- helping people to manage emotional, psychological and social issues, including stress and relaxation;
- additional forms of support such as advising on sources of funding, employment opportunities and applying for financial benefits;
- advice and support for carers.

Occupational therapists work in hospitals and various community settings. Home visits for assessment and advice are a major part of their work. Referral varies – in some areas this may be through the GP or specialist nurse; in others you can refer yourself by contacting your local social services department. Some occupational therapists also work in private practice but you need to make sure that they are state registered (they will have the letters SROT after their name). To find a private occupational therapist contact Occupational Therapists in Independent Practice. For more information on occupational therapists contact the British Association/College of Occupational Therapists.

Dietitians

Dietitians advise people with food-related problems or health conditions where diet is a vital factor in prevention or management, e.g. diabetes, heart disease, obesity and food allergies.

Referral to an NHS dietitian is usually via your GP, specialist or Parkinson's disease nurse specialist. You can also see a dietitian on a private basis but make sure you see a registered dietitian – they will have the letters RD after their name. Contact the British Dietetic Association for more information.

Podiatrists (chiropodists)

Referral to a podiatrist is important for people with many conditions, especially those where care of the feet is important to prevent serious health problems or where circulation or mobility is affected, e.g. diabetes, arthritis or Parkinson's disease.

As well as treating foot problems, podiatrists provide advice on general foot care and problems like corns, callus and in-growing toenails. Podiatrists can also advise on orthoses, tailor-made devices such as shoe inserts or arch supports, used to improve gait and alleviate foot and leg pain.

Podiatrists work in a variety of places, including doctors' surgeries, hospitals, nursing homes and private practice. Home visits can be arranged for people with serious mobility problems. Referral is usually via the GP, a member of his/her primary care team or hospital consultant. Contact the Society of Chiropodists and Podiatrists for more information.

Pharmacists

Coping with medication, especially if it involves a complex regimen involving several drugs, can be very challenging – especially if the person is being treated for other conditions as well – and your pharmacist may be an invaluable source of advice.

Community pharmacists

Community pharmacists often work in a local pharmacy or store. Some are also employed by a primary care trust, local GP surgery or health centre. Their role may include:

- dispensing medicine and ensuring safety;
- checking prescriptions to make sure that the right medicine is taken in the right dose and you have the instructions you need about taking them;
- answering questions about the medication;
- giving advice if swallowing tablets is a problem;
- suggesting pill boxes and timers to people to remember when to take medication;
- recommending ways of opening drug packaging for people who have arthritis and other health conditions that make fine finger movements difficult;
- keeping a computer record of medications;
- providing details about prescription charges – whether you need to pay them and, if you do, how you can obtain a 'prepayment' certificate (or season ticket) for medications you need on a regular basis. This lasts for either four or 12 months and saves you money

if you need more than five items in four months or 14 items in 12 months.

Your local primary care trust will have a list of all local NHS contracted pharmacies. The National Pharmacy Association and the Royal Pharmaceutical Society of Great Britain can also advise.

Hospital pharmacists

Hospital pharmacists are involved in all aspects of the use of medicines within hospitals. They work with medical and nursing staff to ensure that patients are given the most appropriate treatment while in hospital. They might also provide patient-centred advice about treatments, side effects, self-medication and admissions for surgery where you need to be nil-by-mouth but still require essential medication.

Social workers

Social workers help people to find solutions to problems affecting their health, social environment or emotional well-being and may specialize in adult or children/young people's services. Adult services may include working with people in residential care who have mental health problems or learning difficulties; helping older and disabled people to live independently in the community by helping them to access benefits, care services or sheltered housing or planning someone's discharge from hospital so that services are there if they need them when they go home. Children/young people services may include helping families to stay together by providing assistance and advice and helping young carers. Contact the British Association of Social Workers for more information (see Chapter 4: Community care).

Continence services

Managing continence problems is for many carers a major part of their caring role. Although you may find it difficult to raise the subject, considerable help is available, including treatments, products and information. So don't be afraid to discuss this with your GP, who can refer you to a district nurse or a nurse who specializes in continence. They may visit you in your home to discuss any problems, methods of managing these, and any local continence and laundry services that may be available. In many cases you can refer yourself to a continence advisor.

Occupational therapists, physiotherapists and dietitians may also provide advice on aspects of continence care. (See Useful addresses: The Continence Foundation and The Disabled Living Foundation.)

Day hospitals/rehabilitation centres

Day hospitals or rehabilitation centres provide opportunities for assessment by several members of a multidisciplinary team, including physiotherapists, occupational therapists, speech and language therapists, nurses, and doctors, resulting in an individual multidisciplinary care programme – several different disciplines working together to provide care for a person according to his or her needs.

Day hospitals and rehabilitation centres also have links to other disciplines, such as dietitians, podiatrists, psychologists, counsellors and social services. The benefits are that instead of having to see each member of the team separately, you can see them all in one place on the same day. This encourages coordinated care. They also often provide group activities and talks that give you an opportunity to meet other people. Transport can usually be provided if necessary.

Day hospitals and rehabilitation centres also provide support to carers.

Referral criteria will depend on your local area. Your GP, specialist or specialist nurse should be able to advise you further.

Psychiatrists, psychologists and counsellors

Psychiatrists are medical doctors who specialize in psychiatry – the study of mental illness and emotional problems. They can prescribe drugs and other medical treatments, such as electroconvulsive therapy.

Psychologists are not medically trained but have degrees in psychology. They do not prescribe drugs or other medical treatments. Those involved with carers and the people they are caring for are likely to specialize in one of the following areas:

- Clinical psychologists diagnose, assess and treat people with a wide variety of health problems, e.g. depression, anxiety, behavioural disorders, mental illness, and addiction.
- Counselling psychologists see clients in a private and confidential setting to discuss distress or difficulties they are having in their life, e.g. bereavement, relationships, ill health. The aim is to enable

people to see situations more clearly so that they can make choices or changes to their life or accept difficult situations.

- Educational psychologists work with children and young people to assess abilities and assist those who have difficulties with learning or social adjustment. They often work in local education authorities and schools.
- Health psychologists use psychology to promote lifestyle and behavioural change.

Many GP surgeries have counsellors attached to their practice or can provide you with information about other local sources of counselling. There are also several organizations that can provide you with further information, including details of private counsellors (see Useful addresses). The mental health charity, Mind, publishes a comprehensive guide, *Making Sense of Counselling*.

Talking to doctors and healthcare professionals

Don't be afraid to ask your doctor about anything you are concerned about, even if you find it difficult. If they don't know what problems you are having, they cannot help you, and there are solutions to many difficulties. Remember that even if the question is embarrassing, you probably won't be the first person who has asked.

Some people find it helpful to make a list of the things they want to talk about before they see the doctor. Some give it to the doctor when they have their appointment. Keeping a diary can also enable you to keep track of any symptoms, especially if they fluctuate, and help you to describe what is happening to your doctor.

The Patients Association publishes a booklet called 'You and Your Doctor' which gives information on how to get the best out of your doctor.

The website <www.embarrassingproblems.com> includes a section on talking to your doctor about tricky problems.

See also the book *How to Get the Best from Your Doctor* by Dr Tom Smith, published by Sheldon Press.

Age Concern publishes a useful book for older people, *Your Rights to Health Care* by Lorna Easterbrook, which provides information on different NHS services.

Personal experiences

Carers I spoke to while writing this book had very mixed experiences of accessing and dealing with health/social care professionals. Some had found them easy to access and very responsive to their needs. Others had a very difficult time and felt they constantly had to ask and push for services. The experiences of Michael and Sue in Chapter 10: Caring at a distance demonstrate these differences.

Several felt that having someone to coordinate their care made all the difference. This might be any member of the health/social care team, who would act as the main contact point for a disabled/ill person and their family, responding to their needs and coordinating services.

Liz Williams, an occupational therapist by profession, works for a primary care trust in Essex as a case manager for older people with long-term conditions and has a special interest in neurological conditions. Her role demonstrates how this can work.

Liz's job is to provide coordinated, patient-centred care, liaising with health, social services and the voluntary sector in an effort to provide a seamless service, while supporting the patient, family and carers. Community services have expanded in the area with an excellent district nursing service, community physiotherapist and occupational therapist, a collaborative care team and a very active day hospital that provides a falls management programme and an early intervention programme for people with Parkinson's disease.

Liz thinks it is important for patients and carers to be aware of the services that are available and to be able to access these services when needed without prolonged waits and lengthy referral processes. In her role as case manager and advocate for the patient, Liz can access the appropriate services with a minimum of delay.

Providing support to the carer is a key part of her work. A husband or wife might suddenly become a carer – a role they feel ill-prepared to take on. The responsibility of caring, the sheer physical exhaustion and the range of emotions experienced may need to be addressed. Liz says, 'A case manager aims to help carers become more confident in their new role by offering support and practical advice. A great deal is asked of carers – it can be a very isolating role – and I feel every effort must be made to ensure that they feel supported and are aware of the services available to help them.'

4

Community care

Your local social service department is responsible for arranging support services for people who need help to live independently in the community, because of their age, illness or disability. They do this through what is known as a 'needs' or 'care' assessment. The assessment may also identify healthcare requirements that are the responsibility of the local health authority rather than social services, for example a district nurse visiting regularly to administer an injection. Where such needs are identified, social services will inform your GP or another member of your primary care team.

In complex cases, several different health professionals may become involved in the assessment, including therapists, nurses and the GP. The assessment generally takes place in the person's own home and should take into account any personal preferences and requirements that they have as well as their social and cultural background.

Carer's assessments

Since the Carers (Recognition and Services) Act 1995 was implemented, a carer can also ask for his or her own needs to be included in the assessment of the person they care for, and to be taken into account when services are planned for that person, if they are receiving services or if the situation changes and more help is needed.

Under the Carers and Disabled Children Act 2000, a carer is also entitled to have an assessment in his or her own right, even if the person they care for refuses to be assessed. Local authorities can now provide services to carers as well as the person being cared for.

Young people (aged under 18 years) who provide care to adult family members are also entitled to an assessment of their needs, under the Children Act 1989. The local children's department would normally carry this out. Occasionally, children aged 16 or 17 can have a carer's assessment under the Carers and Disabled Children Act 2000 or if under 16, in special situations under the Carers (Recognition and Services) Act 1995.

The carer's assessment can happen at the same time as the main assessment for the person being cared for, or separately. You are entitled to have a friend or advocate present if you feel this would help.

The assessment gives you an opportunity to discuss your situation, how you feel about caring, and what help you need to maintain your own well-being and to manage any other commitments you have. The social worker should explore with you the support and services you might need and what is available – to help both the person you are caring for, and you as a carer. From this, they will draw up a care plan. The services suggested are largely dependent on your area, but might include support in your home to help you with caring tasks or house-work, day care or respite care services to give you a break, equipment or alterations to your house, or opportunities for social contacts and leisure, for example carers' groups.

Carers UK[14] say that local authorities are required to set out their eligibility criteria, i.e. how they make decisions on whether or not to provide services. The needs that are identified in any assessments are compared with these. If the needs of the person you care for match the eligibility criteria, the local authority must provide services to meet their needs. If you want to know what your local authority's eligibility criteria are, contact them and ask them for a copy of their Better Care, Higher Standards Charter.

They also say that social services are only required to meet needs that no one else is willing to meet. Therefore, it is important that if you are unable or unwilling to provide any aspect of caring, that this is taken into account when the local authority is deciding on the services they need to provide. Try to be clear about the level of care you can cope with – for instance, that you are able to provide most of the care so long as you get regular breaks or are able to work.

Social services cannot refuse to meet a need they have identified solely because they do not have the money or other resources required. They should also make it clear to you what has been provided for the person you care for, and what has been given to you.

The person you care for can refuse services, which can mean you have little support. If this is the case, make sure the local authority considers what other services they could provide to you specifically to ease your caring burden – for instance, helping you with cleaning or washing.

Community care and carer's assessments are complex and it is important you seek advice if you do not understand anything about them, if you feel under pressure to accept inadequate services, or you are unhappy with the assessment and how it was carried out. Social services have procedures for dealing with complaints and concerns, which you can access if you feel you have cause. Sources of further information and support include local carers' organizations, Citizens Advice or the helplines run by Carers UK and the Princess Royal Trust for Carers.

You can also contact the social worker for a follow-up visit if you feel there were other aspects of your caring role that were not covered at the time of the assessment. According to the Carers UK website, 'this is quite common – people's lives are often complex and it can be tough to talk about difficult issues regarding close relationships.'[15]

Preparing for an assessment

Preparing for an assessment is very important. Make sure you mention anything that affects your life as a carer. Wherever possible, you should also discuss the assessment with the person you are caring for and agree the points that you want to raise. If there is anything that you want to discuss privately, tell the assessor you would like to speak to him or her confidentially.

Many carers find it helpful to keep a diary of how they cope with caring, their tasks, and anything else concerned with caring that affects them. This can be particularly helpful when preparing for an assessment, applying for benefits, or when visiting the doctor or other healthcare professional. Some carers also find keeping a diary therapeutic, as it helps them keep track of their situation and provides an outlet for their feelings. What you put in the diary depends very much on your own individual situation, but you should be as honest as possible and include anything you feel is relevant or that causes you great difficulty. The Parkinson's Disease Society produces an information sheet called 'Keeping a Diary: For carers' (available on its website) which, although written for carers of people with Parkinson's, outlines aspects relevant to any carer.

The section on carer's assessments on the Carers UK website also provides a checklist of aspects to consider when preparing for an assessment – these include:

- housing
- health
- work
- leisure interests
- time spent caring
- feelings

- relationships
- emergencies
- the future.

Don't assume that health professionals will automatically suggest a carer's assessment to you. A sad fact of life is that many carers do not know they are entitled to an assessment, and many healthcare professionals never mention it. If you think you could benefit from one, ask for one. You do this by contacting your local social services. The phone number will be listed in your local telephone directory under the local authority or your GP surgery should be able to provide you with the details. If the person you are caring for is in hospital, ask someone at the hospital to put you in touch with a hospital social worker.

Some carers are wrongly told that they are not entitled to an assessment. If this happens to you, do write to your social services and ask why you have been refused an assessment. You can also seek advice from a local carers' organization or Citizens Advice.

Paying for care

Although the assessment is free, who pays for services depends on your financial situation and the eligibility criteria for service provision in your area. This will usually be means-tested and depend on a financial assessment, which is often completed by the care manager or social worker at the same time as the needs or carer's assessment. If you do not provide this information, social services may assume you can pay the full cost of the services.

The charges made will vary, but every social services department must ensure:[16]

- the charges are 'reasonable';
- people are only charged what they can afford;
- that someone doesn't experience hardship or is denied a service needed as a result of them not being able to pay;
- that the extra costs that a person incurs as a result of a disability, ill health or caring is taken into account;
- that charges are reduced or dropped that would cause hardship to the person;
- they do not take into account Disability Living Allowance mobility component.

The local authority may be able to offer you financial support if you need it, provided you meet their eligibility criteria, and should also be able to advise on other sources of financial help.

Direct payments[17]

Direct payments are cash payments that are sometimes given by a local authority in lieu of social service provisions, to people who have been assessed as needing services. They can be made to:

- disabled people aged 16 or over;
- people with parental responsibility for disabled children;
- carers aged 16 or over in respect of carer services.

The idea behind direct payments is to give people more flexibility in how services are provided to them. Giving money instead of social care services provides people with greater choice and control over the delivery of their care. How much money is provided will depend on the assessed person's financial means.

A note of caution about paying for care

Paying for care, in the home and in hospital and residential settings, is a complex issue, which is subject to change and differs depending on where in the UK you live. There have been also many worrying reports in the media about the state of the NHS, social services and paying for long-term care. It is impossible to comment on these ongoing political situations in this book. Try not to get too worried by what you read in the paper but make sure you get expert advice relevant to your particular circumstances. Social services, Citizens Advice, Age Concern, Counsel and Care as well as carers or health-condition-specific voluntary organizations should be able to advise further.

Further information

Carers UK and the Princess Royal Trust for Carers websites contain useful information on community care and carer's assessments. Local carers' organizations or centres can also advise you further. Carers UK publishes 'Looking After Someone: A guide to carers' rights and benefits in each UK county', which covers practical and financial help as well as combining work and caring.

The Royal Association for Disability and Rehabilitation (RADAR) publishes a book called *If Only I'd Known That a Year Ago*, edited by John Stanford, which provides an introduction to services, rights and facilities.

The Commission for Social Care Inspection is the single, independent inspectorate for all social care services in England. It promotes improvements in social care for the benefit of people who use care services. There is a wealth of information on social care on its website and you can also get advice from its helpline. There are also similar organizations in Scotland (the Scottish Commission for the Regulation of Care), Wales (Care Standards Inspectorate for Wales), and Northern Ireland (the Regulation and Quality Improvement Authority).

CareAware is a non-profitmaking public information and advisory service specializing in long-term care for older people. It has information and a helpline that can provide personal and individual assistance.

Equipment

A wide range of aids and equipment is available to help people who have disabilities or ill health, though you need to ensure they are truly suitable, and they can be very expensive.

If you are considering buying equipment to help you with day-to-day living, it is important that you first obtain an assessment from the relevant therapist, who can assess your needs and then make recommendations, including equipment if they think it will help with a particular problem. Without this assessment, you run the risk of spending considerable sums on equipment that may prove to be unsuitable or could have been purchased for a much cheaper price. If therapists do suggest something, they should be able to advise you on suppliers and funding.

What kind of therapist you see depends on what particular activity you need help with. There is inevitable overlap between the disciplines, although they often work together as part of a team. In general:

- an occupational therapist will advise on activities of daily living such as washing, bathing, dressing, eating, reading and leisure;
- a physiotherapist would advise on mobility problems inside and outside the house. This is complicated, however, by the fact that an occupational therapist will often also advise on equipment such as wheelchairs;
- a speech and language therapist will advise on anything to do with communication and on swallowing problems.

Your GP, hospital doctor or Patient Advisory and Liaison Service should be able to advise you further. See Chapter 3: Healthcare professionals, or see the Disabled Living Foundation in Useful addresses.

Who pays for the equipment depends on the type of equipment in question, your particular circumstances (e.g. whether you are on benefits), and the funding available in your local area or from other sources. Your therapist, GP or hospital doctor should be able to tell you what is available. The Disabled Living Foundation has an information sheet, 'Sources of Funding and Obtaining Equipment for Disabled and Older People', which can be downloaded from their website or ordered by post.

Unsolicited doorstep/telephone sales

Although many equipment manufacturers and sellers are honourable, there have been reports of some rogue traders who target vulnerable people, through unsolicited doorstep and telephone calls. They often use persuasive and sometimes aggressive tactics to encourage them to purchase equipment that is expensive and may not be suitable for their needs. The Office of Fair Trading website has further information <www.oft.gov.uk/Consumer/Doorstep+selling/>.

Community alarm systems

If you are caring for someone who spends time alone while you are out at work, etc. or you are caring at a distance for someone who lives on their own, one of your main concerns might be how to ensure that they can summon help if they have a fall or accident. A community alarm system might be a solution. These are run by many local authorities as well as voluntary organizations such as Age Concern and Help the Aged.

When a person registered with one of these schemes has an accident, they can push a button on their phone or a device worn around their wrist or neck to summon help from a 24-hour response centre. A modest fee is charged for most of these systems but there are usually exemptions for some people who are on low incomes. Your social services department will be able to advise you on what is available.

Computers

Many people with disabilities and carers have found that having a computer has made an enormous difference to their lives, not only to help them with day-to-day business and letters, but also to help them keep in touch with other people, and obtain information from the Internet. Online shopping and banking can also make a lot of difference to people who have problems with mobility.

Occupational therapists can advise on getting a computer or an electronic typewriter and any funding available. You can also obtain information and support from AbilityNet, a voluntary organization that aims to make computer technology accessible to people who have disabilities.

Colleges and adult education facilities in your local area may also run computer courses. Further details can be obtained from your local library or your local authority education office. Support for disabled students should also be available. (See Chapter 6: Employment and education for carers.)

Adaptations to your home

You may also find that you need to have repairs or adaptations made to your home to accommodate the person you are caring for. This might include improving access in and out of your front door by providing a ramp, refitting a bathroom to make it easier to manage or fitting a stair lift.

Before going ahead with any work like this, seek professional advice from an occupational therapist. He or she can assess the difficulties you are having and make proper recommendations accordingly.

Another source of information and advice is Care and Repair. They produce a useful guide, 'In Good Repair', which provides information on repairs, adaptations, funding and finding a reliable builder or tradesman. Advice can also be obtained from the Disabled Living Foundation and the Centre for Accessible Environments (see Useful addresses).

Transport

Driving

If the person you are caring for is still able to drive after the diagnosis of a significant health condition or disability (e.g. Parkinson's disease, multiple sclerosis) they have two legal obligations:

1 They must inform the Driver and Vehicle Licensing Agency (DVLA) in writing. The DVLA will send them a PK1 form (application for

a driving licence/notification of driving licence holder's state of health). In most cases, the DVLA will receive sufficient information from the person's doctor to decide whether or not to issue them with a licence for three years, after which they will review the circumstances. In some cases additional information may be required. This usually involves a driving ability test at a driving assessment centre.

They should share any concerns they have about driving with their doctor. The UK also has several specialized driving and mobility centres that provide assessments information and advice about adaptations to make driving easier.

2 They must tell their insurance company. It is illegal to drive on public roads in the UK without at least third party insurance, and failure to tell the insurers is likely to invalidate your insurance. Many people are reluctant to tell their insurers because they are afraid that they will be forced to stop driving or end up with increased premiums. This may not be the case. If it is, some insurers specialize in insuring disabled drivers. The organizations listed at the end of this section should be able to advise further.

There is also a legal duty to report any later changes in driving ability to the DVLA and the insurance company.

If the person you are caring for is on the higher rate of the mobility component of Disability Living Allowance (DLA – see Chapter 5: Finances) or has a war pension, they may be able to obtain some help from Motability, which provides mobility solutions for disabled people on these benefits. It allows people with disabilities to use the higher rate mobility component of their DLA or war pensioners' mobility supplement to buy or hire a car. Motability offers two types of scheme – hiring and hire purchase. Under the hire purchase scheme, it is possible to buy an electric wheelchair or good used car as well as a new one.

Parking

The Blue Badge scheme is designed to help blind people and those with severe mobility problems by allowing them to park close to shops, public buildings and other places. It applies throughout England, Scotland and Wales, with the exception of four central London areas – the City of London, Westminster, Kensington and Chelsea and part of Camden. Application is usually through your local housing or social services office or the town hall. The Blue Badge is automatically awarded to a person who is in receipt of the high rate mobility component of DLA.

National Key Scheme for Disabled Toilets

The Royal Association for Disability and Rehabilitation (RADAR) initiated the national key scheme for disabled toilets in the 1970s. Although it is preferable for all disabled toilets to be kept unlocked, unfortunately many have to be locked to maintain cleanliness and protect them from vandalism and misuse. RADAR's National Key Scheme offers people with disabilities independent access to over 4,000 locked public toilets around Britain.

Keys cost £3.50 each including postage and packing. To obtain one you need to write to RADAR with your name and address and a declaration in writing confirming your disability (in order to claim VAT exemption on the key). RADAR also produces a National Key Scheme Guide (price £8.00 including postage and packing), which lists over 4,000 accessible toilets throughout the UK. RADAR can also provide information on many other aspects of living with a disability.

Public transport

If the person you are caring for relies on public transport to get around, there are several initiatives that may help.

The Disability Discrimination Acts 1995 and 2004 give the government powers to make regulations relating to the design of and access to newly built public transport vehicles such as buses, taxis, coaches, trains and trams. This is to ensure that disabled people can use them.

They may also be entitled to a Disabled Person's Railcard, which entitles them and an accompanying adult to one-third off the price of a rail ticket. Eligibility criteria and application forms are available from main stations or from the Disabled Persons Railcard Office.

Local authorities also have discretionary powers to operate concessionary fares for people with disabilities. This might include a bus or travel pass. For more information on what is available in your area, contact your local authority public transport information office, whose number should be in the phone book or available from the local Citizens Advice office.

Further sources of information on transport issues

The Forum of Mobility Centres, which offers advice and information to individuals with medical conditions or who have an injury that may affect driving

The Disabled Persons Transport Advisory Committee (DPTAC) advises the government on the transport needs of all disabled people and has a transport and travel website for disabled and less mobile people called 'Door to Door'. See <www.dptac.gov.uk>.

Mobilise is a self-help organization run for disabled people by disabled people, which provides information and campaigns on all aspects of mobility, including driving, wheelchairs and public transport.

Ricability, an independent research charity, produces reports and fact sheets on disability issues, including guides for motorists with particular needs.

Disability discrimination

The Disability Discrimination Acts 1995 and 2004 protect disabled people from discrimination in several areas, including:

● employment
● education
● access to goods
● facilities and services and buying or renting land or property.

More information is available from the Disability Rights Commission, which can also advise anyone who has experienced discrimination. The government website <www.direct.gov.uk> also has information on the Acts.

Acknowledgement

Much of the information in this chapter on carers' assessments is based on information published on the Carers UK and the Princess Royal Trust for Carers websites.

5
Finances

It is natural to worry about money – most carers do. Research by the social policy research and development charity, Joseph Rowntree Foundation[18] and Contact a Family/The Family Fund[19] (voluntary organizations for families who have a disabled child) has shown that disability can have a significant impact on finances and debt. As well as incurring extra costs in order to manage the disability or illness, household incomes can be considerably reduced as a result of someone being disabled or a carer. For example, it is estimated that bringing up a disabled child costs three times what it costs to raise another child.

The financial concerns you are likely to have and the help available to you will depend on:

- your specific circumstances and resources;
- what stage you are at in your life;
- whom you are caring for and the help he or she needs;
- what your caring role involves.

If you are a younger carer, your priorities might be earning a living, paying the mortgage, raising your family and saving for a pension. If you are older, you may have paid off your mortgage and no longer be working, but you may be worried about how you are going to stretch your pension to cover the extra costs of caring.

This chapter provides a very brief overview of some of these financial issues. It does not provide detailed information on all the benefits and help that may be available. This is because the subjects covered are very complicated and the benefits/legal systems are subject to frequent change. Instead, it identifies resources and organizations that can provide you with the expert advice you need to ensure that you access the financial help available to you and the person you are caring for. There is also a brief guide to power of attorney, something you should know about if your caring role includes (or may in the future) managing the financial affairs of the person you care for.

Even if you don't feel you need any assistance at the moment, planning for the future is crucial. Therefore, try to obtain as much information and advice on the options or support that may be available to you, now and at a later date.

Some people find it hard to accept welfare benefits because they perceive these as 'charity'. If this is how you feel, remember that you will most likely have paid for these benefits via your taxes for years. Many people (with disabilities and carers) have told me that receiving even a little extra financial help has made a huge difference to their quality of life.

For information about paying for care services, see Chapter 4: Community care.

Welfare benefits

For people who are ill or have disabilities

Disability benefits are non-means tested and are one of the ways of providing extra income for people with a long-term illness or a disability like Parkinson's.

The two disability benefits are called Disability Living Allowance (DLA) and Attendance Allowance (AA).

Men and women who are under the age of 65 when they make a first claim may claim DLA. People who are still working can claim it. This has two parts:

- *A care component* paid to people who need help with personal care or to watch over them to ensure they are safe. There are three rates depending on the amount of care or supervision needed.
- *A mobility component* for people who have difficulty walking out of doors. This has two rates depending on a person's level of need.

Attendance Allowance is for people who make a first claim after the age of 65. There are two rates depending on the amount of help needed with personal care or supervision.

If either of these disability benefits is awarded, then extra income entitlement may be generated through other welfare benefits. It is important that anyone given a disability benefit should get an income maximization check carried out by a member of the Department for Work and Pensions or a qualified adviser in an organization like Citizens Advice.

Disabled children

The rules regarding welfare benefits and other financial resources for disabled/ill children are different from those for adults. Organizations that provide support to children and their families with the specific disability or illness your child has should be able to provide you with advice and information – examples include Scope (cerebral palsy), the National Autistic Society and the Muscular Dystrophy Association.

Contact a Family produces a comprehensive guide, 'Benefits, Tax Credits and Other Financial Help – UK', which provides an overview of all the main benefits and tax credits available, but focuses on those aspects that most affect families with disabled children. Its helpline can also provide advice.

The Family Fund provides financial grants to families with severely disabled or ill children aged 15 and under, provided they are resident in the UK and meet the fund's criteria.

For carers

Carer's Allowance is a taxable financial benefit available to informal carers, aged 16 years or over, who regularly spend more than 35 hours a week caring for someone (a relative, friend or neighbour) who is severely disabled and receiving either Attendance Allowance or Disability Living Allowance (care component at the middle or higher rate). This can, however, affect the level of other benefits and entitlements that you may be getting.

Carers of working age are often worried about how caring will affect their state pension, especially if they are unable to work or have a low income. The government has made provisions to protect carers' rights to a state pension and provide other financial support for those in retirement, such as Pension Credit.

Other benefits may also be available, depending on your circumstances. The Department for Work and Pensions, a local carers' centre or a Citizens Advice bureau should be able to advise further.

Other sources of financial assistance

Financial assistance and other forms of support can sometimes be obtained from other sources, provided you meet their specific criteria. These include trade unions, professional organizations, benevolent funds (such as those tied to the armed services or to particular professions), national/local charitable trusts as well as religious and cultural associations.

There are several publications that can help you locate these. The Disabled Living Foundation has a fact sheet, 'Sources of Funding and Obtaining Equipment for Disabled and Older People'. The Directory of Social Change has a directory called *A Guide to Grants for Individuals in Need*. You may also find it helpful to contact Charity Search, an organization that provides information on sources of funding for older people.

The Association of Charity Officers has a helpline that can signpost enquirers to charities most likely to be able to offer them help. It also has a special interest group network for charities that provide support services for people with connections to particular industries, trades and professions called the Occupational Benevolent Funds Alliance.

See also the resources listed in the voluntary organizations section of Chapter 2: Sources of information and advice.

Further information and advice on financial matters

Information is available from the Department for Work and Pensions, which has several delivery organizations. For most people, the two key ones are Jobcentre Plus for people of working age and the Pension Service for people aged over 60. Both departments produce excellent resources that are available from their local offices or on the Department for Work and Pensions website.

Other organizations that provide advice include Citizens Advice (see Chapter 2: Sources of information and advice), Age Concern and local authority welfare rights units. Their offices in your area should be listed in your telephone directory. Many voluntary organizations dealing with specific health conditions should also be able to advise further.

The Princess Royal Trust for Carers and Carers UK have useful information about carers and money on their websites.

The government's Directgov website <www.direct.gov.uk/caring forsomeone/moneymatters> has a comprehensive guide to financial management and caring, which I have used extensively as a resource for this chapter.

Debt

In November 2006, Citizens Advice reported that it had advised on 1.4 million debt problems during 2005–6, an 11 per cent increase on the previous year. During this time period, one-fifth of people asking them for advice were seeking help with debt problems.[20]

Debt can be a particular hazard for people who are disabled, ill or caring. The reasons vary but can include being unable to cope with the sheer cost of disability or caring, having to meet unexpected expenses and difficulties making ends meet on a reduced household income.

If for any reason you find yourself in debt, please don't despair but seek help from the many sources of debt advice available. Your local Citizens Advice should be able to advise you further. The Citizens Advice website, <www.adviceguide.org.uk>, has a useful section on dealing with debt.

The National Debtline provides free, confidential and independent telephone advice to people with debt problems in England, Wales and Scotland. It can also help you to set up a debt management plan, if your circumstances meet certain criteria.

Contact a Family produces comprehensive, accessible guides for families of disabled children about dealing with debt in England and Wales, Scotland and Northern Ireland

Power of attorney

Sometimes, a person being cared for is unable to manage his or her legal and financial affairs, and may need to appoint someone (e.g. a relative, friend or professional) to act on their behalf – this is known as 'Power of Attorney'.

Another form of this, Enduring Power of Attorney (EPA), can also be taken out while the person is still capable of managing their affairs. This is not enforced until needed but involves someone being appointed to manage a person's affairs should he or she become incapable of doing this in the future. 'Lasting Power of Attorney', a new type that will replace EPA, allows the person to choose someone to make decisions about personal welfare as well as financial matters when he or she is unable to do this.

The Public Guardianship Office is responsible for ensuring that someone is appointed to look after the financial affairs of people who are not mentally capable of doing so themselves. They provide information on power of attorney on their website or through their customer services helpline.

The Citizens Advice website <www.adviceguide.org.uk> has a useful guide to managing financial affairs for someone else in England, Wales and Northern Ireland. Their local bureaux could also advise you further.

In Scotland, power of attorney falls under the Adults with Incapacity (Scotland) Act 2000. More information is available from the Scottish Executive website <www.scotland.gov.uk> or from Scottish mental health organizations such as Alzheimer Scotland – Action on Dementia.

Wills

A common concern for many carers is how to leave money to the person who is being cared for in a will to ensure their welfare and financial security after the carer dies. This is a complicated issue that can involve bodies such as the Public Guardianship Office (see above) or the Court of Protection (which is responsible for the assets and monies of people who are unable to manage their own affairs due to mental incapacity). There are several options that you can consider but it is vital that you consult a solicitor, preferably one that specializes in this area of law, for further advice.

Mencap has a guide to leaving money to people with a learning disability, 'Leaving Money by Will', which can help you consider the issues involved. The Disability Law Service is a law and advisory voluntary organization that provides confidential and free legal advice for disabled adults, their families and carers. It specializes in six areas of law:

- consumer contract
- community care
- disability discrimination
- education
- employment
- welfare benefits.

It publishes several information sheets, including 'Guidelines for Trusts where there is a Member of the Family with a Disability' (stamped addressed envelope required).

Personal experiences

Eva and Robin

For the past two years, Clare, the daughter of Eva and Robin (profiled in Chapter 1: What is a carer?), has been living in her own bungalow, about 15 minutes' drive from her parents' home, with 24-hour support from carers paid for with direct payments (see pp. 41–3). To enable her to do this, her parents have taken the unusual step of setting up their own housing association – where they paid the capital. Now Clare, with the help of a specialist mortgage company, has a 100 per cent mortgage on part of the bungalow and pays rent on the proportion that the housing association owns. Fortunately, because the bungalow was being built at the time they purchased it, they were able to make adaptations before it was completed.

With the help of her parents, Clare chooses her own carers, who work shifts. Eva and Robin are involved in recruiting, advertising, interviewing, and ensuring that proper contracts of employment are drawn up and that everything conforms to employment law. Eva says, 'Direct payments tend to be presented as a positive thing because you can have what you want. To some extent this is true because you recruit your own carers who work for you and you can pay them a reasonable wage. However, you couldn't afford to get all the caring support from agencies, but that wouldn't have been appropriate in our case anyway. It is time-consuming and you need to know what you are doing.'

When one of the carers leaves, Eva has to take on their shifts until a replacement is found, although turnover hasn't been too frequent. She adds, 'I admire the fact that Clare can accept other people are going to do the most intimate things for her. That's why it is important to get the right carers. There is a certain amount of emotional investment on both sides because the carers have to know her as a person and are in her home. Their job is to help her live the life she would live if she could do things for herself.'

Eva's greatest fear is what will happen to Clare when she and Robin are no longer around to help her. They have received expert advice on wills and trusts to ensure her welfare in this event. Clare has a brother, Dan, who does what he can to help but is married with a full-time job. 'He would do anything for her,' Eva explains, 'but I would not ask him to because I don't want him to do what we have done. His life has been compromised by the fact that his sister is disabled, although he has never complained and we have done our best to ensure that we have had times specifically for him. I accept that we have to do what we have to do as Clare's parents, but I wouldn't wish it on my worst enemy so I certainly don't wish it on my son whom I love.'

6

Employment and education for carers

Work is an important part of our lives. As well as being a means of earning a living, it provides us with a sense of identity, fulfilment and social interaction. Of the six million carers in the UK, it is estimated that three million combine caring with paid work.[21] For example, a recent staff survey carried out by Barclays Bank, which has more than 84,000 employees in the UK, revealed that more than half of their staff had caring responsibilities.[22]

Unfortunately, carers can face many barriers to employment. These include finding an understanding employer as well as good quality, flexible and affordable alternative care; bridging the gap between benefits and work; and loss of confidence/work skills if they have had to give up work to care for someone.

Recognition of the needs of carers with respect to employment and education is growing and two recent government acts have given carers new rights. The Carers (Equal Opportunities) Act 2004 that came into force in April 2005 aims to ensure that carers can take up working, studying and leisure opportunities. The Work and Families Act 2006, taking effect in April 2007, gives carers new rights (that parents of children aged under six and disabled children aged under 18 already have) to request flexible working from their employer. Hopefully this legislation will greatly improve the employment opportunities available to carers.

Making employment and education opportunities more accessible to carers also has many benefits for employers and for the economy.

Action on Carers and Employment

According to Carers UK, employers who grant flexible working rights to carers have a more productive workforce, with lower staff turnover and a reduction in sick leave. This organization is the lead partner in an initiative called Action on Carers and Employment (ACE), part-funded by the European Social Fund's Equal programme, which aims to raise awareness of the barriers facing carers who want to work and support the inclusion of carers in training and work.

The project's objectives are to:

- carry out research into the factors that influence why, how and if carers access alternative care services that enable them to work;
- use delivery partnerships (i.e. organizations working together to carry out the work and/or put services into place) to identify and enhance existing care services, and develop and test new care services, which enable carers to work;
- support the participation of carers in planning the development and delivery of care service provision;
- develop a national policy partnership that will use the lessons of the research and delivery partnerships to influence long-term development and investment in the health and social care sector, including working to establish a national care strategy.

More information is available on the ACE National Partnership website, <www.acecarers.org.uk> or from Carers UK.

An ACE-led partnership, Employers for Carers, has also been set up to:

- identify and promote the business benefits of supporting carers in the workplace;
- influence employment policy and practice to create a culture that supports carers who are in work and those who want to find employment.

Employers involved in this scheme include British Telecom, civil service departments, HSBC Bank, PriceWaterhouseCoopers and the Metropolitan Police. Steps they have taken include identifying carers in their workforce and developing policies that promote flexible working. The partnership's website <www.carersuk.org/Employersforcarers> contains information, case studies and practical assessment tools to help other employers benefit from this project's findings. It also provides information for carers in employment or thinking of returning to work.

Working Families promotes work–life balance for working parents and carers and helps employers to implement policies that encourage this. As well as general support on employment issues through their publications and helpline, they have a guide, 'Make it Work for You', and a network called Waving not Drowning to support parents who are trying to combine paid work with caring for a disabled child.

Further information and advice

If you are already working, and find combining caring and employment difficult, the first step is to talk to your employer. They may have 'carer-friendly' policies or be interested in developing them. This might include giving time off for emergencies, flexible or part-time hours, working at home, career breaks and job share.[23] Some of the following resources may provide both you and your employer with information.

Your local Jobcentre Plus, the government agency that advises people of working age on employment and benefits, will be able to provide you with support – see <www.jobcentreplus.gov.uk> (see also Chapter 5: Finances).

Carers UK's publication for carers, 'Juggling and Work', provides comprehensive information on carers' employment issues as well as case studies and examples of support that employers have put into practice.

If for any reason you experience discrimination in the workplace because of your caring responsibilities, contact your national or local carers' organization for advice. They can also help you if you currently do not work and would like to consider the options open to you, or if you work and feel your caring responsibilities may mean you have to stop.

The Social Care Institute for Excellence, an organization that aims to improve the experience of people who use social care by developing and promoting good practice in the sector, has produced a comprehensive guide to implementing the Carers (Equal Opportunities) Act 2004 – see <www.scie.org.uk/publications/practiceguides/carers guidance/index.asp>.

Education

The education needs of carers may include:

- practical training on aspects of caring, such as manual handling, planning and advocacy;
- vocational courses to help them improve their employment prospects;
- personal development and leisure.

The Expert Patient Programme Community Interest Company is the government's NHS-based training initiative, which recognizes the importance of patient empowerment. A definition of 'expert patients' is 'people living with a long-term health condition, who are able to take more control over their health by understanding and managing their conditions, leading to an improved quality of life'. It is developing programmes for carers in some areas. These include:

- Looking After Me – for people who care for someone living with a long-term health condition or disability. The course aims to help carers look after themselves, take more control of their situation and make a difference to their life. The trained tutors have experience themselves of caring for a relative.
- The Supporting Parents Programme – a six-week, self-care support course for parents and guardians of children who have long-term and life-limiting conditions. The aim is to provide a space where parents can support each other in dealing with the common problems they face. At least one of the trained facilitators is a parent themselves.

More information can be obtained from the Expert Patient Programme Community Interest Company enquiry line or website <www.expert-patients.nhs.uk>.

City and Guilds, one of the UK's leading providers of vocational qualifications, has developed an online learning resource for carers, called 'Learning for Living' <www.learning-for-living.co.uk>. This is the first e-learning programme of its kind in Europe and aims to provide carers with the confidence and support they need to take up new learning and work opportunities. It leads to a qualification, the 'Certificate in Personal Development and Learning for Unpaid Carers'.

Health and social care professionals may also be able to provide courses on some issues surrounding carers. In particular, physiotherapists or occupational therapists may run courses on manual handling aspects for carers to ensure safety and avoid back injuries. They will also advise carers at home or in rehabilitation/day centre or hospital settings on aspects of caring that are especially relevant to their particular circumstances. See also Chapter 3: Healthcare professionals and Chapter 4: Community care.

Many carers' centres run courses on aspects related to caring and also help carers with employment and education opportunities. The Princess Royal Trust for Carers provides bursaries to carers who are caring or have stopped caring in the past six months to be used for education, personal development, pleasure or skills for returning to work.

In terms of education that provides wider vocational and leisure opportunities, some colleges provide support to carers, so ask any you have an interest in studying with what they offer.

Learndirect <www.learndirect.co.uk> provides a wide range of online courses and has a network of centres across the UK where you can get support. It can also provide information on opportunities elsewhere.

The National Extension College (NEC), a distance-learning college that helps people of all ages fit learning into their lives, offers flexible courses that can be studied where and when you choose. With lottery funding, it also runs a 'Carers into Education Project' with the Princess Royal Trust for Carers to enable carers living in Eastern England and the Midlands to access NEC courses at reduced rates. See <www.nec.ac .uk>.

Other sources of help

Some voluntary organizations provide publications and support on employment and education – for you and, where possible, the person you are caring for. For example, as well as providing information on employment for people with multiple sclerosis (MS), the MS Society's website <www.mssociety.org.uk> has a comprehensive carers' section with advice and useful links. It also has a Carers' Opportunities Fund to provide grants to carers of people with MS.

The government website <www.direct.gov.uk> has information on employment and other carers' issues.

Finding alternative care

Finding alternative care while you work or study should be considered in your carer's assessment (See Chapter 4: Community care). Social services or a carers' organization should also be able to advise you further. Some carers say that finding 'fit for purpose' care can prove difficult. It is to be hoped that the new Carers (Equal Opportunities) Act 2004 will lead to improved services in this respect.

Personal experiences

When Sue was caring at a distance for her elderly father, she worked for a civil service department that had 'family friendly policies' for staff with caring responsibilities. This made a considerable difference to her in terms of feeling secure about combining her job with the caring responsibilities and allowed her to spend time in Yorkshire on occasions when he was hospitalized or ill. She found it helpful to discuss her needs with her welfare department at work, and felt that they would have helped her to find other sources of information/support if she had required assistance.

7

Emotional, psychological and spiritual impact

For many carers, it is the emotional, psychological and spiritual effects of caring that are the hardest aspects to deal with. No matter how much they love the person they are caring for, it is common to have complex, conflicting and fluctuating emotions, including anger and resentment at the restrictions that caring places on their life. Lack of recognition doesn't help, especially if healthcare professionals and visitors only ask about the person being cared for and the carer feels taken for granted.

There is no right or wrong way to 'feel' – so don't be ashamed if you have negative emotions or find caring hard. However, having an outlet to express them is vital.

The first step may be to find someone to talk to. This may be a partner, a relative or friend, who knows you well and with whom you feel comfortable. Or you may prefer to discuss your feelings with someone who is not so closely involved in your life – especially if you don't want to upset someone close or are afraid of the reaction they might have. Examples may be a health or social care professional or helplines/support groups run by voluntary or carers' organizations.

Another alternative is a professional counsellor, to help you look at your life and the feelings you have in a safe environment. Counselling is not about giving advice but providing space and time to explore your feelings and behaviour so you can gain insight into what you find most difficult and why. This can help you to resolve your feelings, accept your situation or make changes to your life. (To access a counsellor see Chapter 3: Healthcare professionals.)

Support from other carers

For most carers, the support of others in a similar position is the key to their ability to survive. There are many ways to make contact with other carers, often through voluntary or carer organizations, including meetings, telephone links or online forums.

Sometimes people are reluctant to join support groups because they are afraid they will meet people who are worse off than them and this frightens them because they think it is how they will be in the future. Try to avoid comparing how you are coping with another's experience. Remember that each person being cared for, and each carer, is different – your experiences may differ, and one approach to caring is not necessarily better than another. Also, advances in medicine, technology and management are being made all the time and these may have a bearing on treatment available to you and the person you are caring for at a later date.

An example of a carer's group is the Harrow branch of Mencap. Members are mainly parents/carers of people with learning disabilities, including autism and Down's syndrome. The meetings often include speakers on carers' issues and opportunities for the carers to talk to each other and share experiences in an informal way. Carers there told me the group provided:

- moral support
- confidence
- friends who understand
- recognition of my caring role
- a lessening of isolation
- general information
- information on benefits and services
- a place to ask for help
- opportunities to share their experiences
- 'time for myself'.

Ruth, who cares for her daughter Alice and volunteers as a local parent representative for Contact a Family, says, 'Talking to someone in a similar position was what I wanted when my daughter was first diagnosed. That's what most of the people who phone me also want. It's about having a common bond and not having to explain to someone about things because they have been through something similar.'

Creative outlets

Finding a creative or relaxing outlet that allows you to express yourself and your feelings may also help. This might include writing, music, art, complementary therapies or exercise.

One of the reasons that Hugh Marriott (see the end of this chapter) gives for deciding to write a book on caring is that 'clattering away at my keyboard would be a positive pleasure and qualify as respite care'.[24]

Anne says she gained a great deal of comfort from being able to play the oboe in a local orchestra while caring for her daughter, Anna.

Relationships

Being a carer can change many aspects of your life and there is no doubt that family relationships can become very strained as a result. Your relationship to the person you are caring for and how this is affected by their disability or illness is a key part of this, as is their attitude towards being cared for. Some carers feel they bear the brunt of the 'dependent' person's emotions – even if they know that these are not really aimed at them personally, but result from the difficulties and frustrations of their illness or disability.

Reversal of roles is common and this can be difficult for both parties to deal with. For instance, the carer may have to take on more domestic chores or become the main breadwinner. They may then feel they have too many responsibilities and feel very stressed. At the same time, the person being cared for may feel bereaved, powerless and lacking in self-esteem because he or she is no longer able to fulfil former roles. This in turn can lead to resentment which may be taken out on their carer simply because he or she is the closest at hand. Role reversal tensions can be common between spouses/partners, and when an adult child is looking after an elderly parent.

Other contributing factors may include increased social isolation because both people are unable to participate in social activities; tiredness; and conflict between family members towards the disability/ illness and how it should be managed.

Sexual relationships

If the person you are caring for is your partner, your sexual relationship may be affected by physical and health factors. In some cases it may be possible to overcome some of these so you can continue to have an intimate life, even if changes have to be made. Psychological issues such as stress, loss of self-esteem, fatigue and depression can also affect sexual relationships. Sometimes both parties can get so caught up in managing the illness in question that they find it hard to focus on their relationship.

Some health conditions affect a person's ability to communicate effectively, especially through facial expression and body language.

This can cause misunderstandings about the affected person's desires and feelings. Some health conditions also affect sexual desire and performance.

Often the answer lies in talking about these matters with your partner, something many people find difficult. Advice may also be available from your doctor or social care professionals, although this can be hard to initiate. Some people have tried and have been put off by a negative response. If this happens to you, try to find someone else to help you. Most professionals should be supportive and help you access any support that may be beneficial such as psychosexual counselling. If you feel too shy or find it too hard to verbalize your concerns, try giving your doctor or other healthcare professional a written list of questions. Some voluntary organizations publish information resources on this subject that you may find helpful.

In some cases, due to the nature of the health condition, there is no possibility of a continued sex life. If this is your situation, and you are finding this difficult, you may find it helpful to discuss it further with an appropriate healthcare professional or counsellor. You may also find it helpful to read Hugh Marriott's book, *The Selfish Pig's Guide to Caring* (see the end of this chapter), which discusses this subject from a carer's perspective.

Diagnosis

The diagnosis of the illness or disability that makes someone a carer is a particularly emotionally challenging time for most people. The stress can be made worse if obtaining a diagnosis is difficult or, as happens in some cases, no conclusive diagnosis is possible.

The manner in which the diagnosis is given, and the additional support provided, is an extremely important factor. Although the diagnosis may be handled sensitively and considerately, some carers find it is handled very badly, causing unnecessary extra stress. With some health conditions, the importance of the 'telling' of the diagnosis has been recognized by healthcare professionals and procedures are being put into place to provide more support at this crucial stage. This includes providing written information and phone numbers, because most people don't take in much information when they are told the diagnosis; setting up a second appointment with a member of the healthcare team at a later date; and identifying a key worker to be their future link person.

Any prior knowledge or experience you have of the condition in question will affect any expectations that you have of the future. If this was some years ago, remember that advances in the understanding, treatment, care and support of many conditions are being made every day and the situation may be very different now.

How the person you are caring for reacts is also important. Some automatically assume that they will become very disabled and have to give up everything they love in life to take on an 'invalid's' role. Others deny that there is anything wrong with them and try to cope without any help, even when they have considerable difficulties that require treatment or management. Both responses can have an impact on the carer.

If you do not receive the information or support you need at the time of diagnosis, Chapter 2: Sources of information and advice provides details of some key information sources you could try, and Chapter 3: Healthcare professionals and Chapter 4: Community care give an overview of health and social care services that may be able to help. Don't wait for someone to suggest something to you; if you think you could benefit from a service or information resource, ask what is available.

Depression and/or burnout

For some carers, the burden of caring that they are carrying becomes too much to bear, resulting in depression and/or burnout. If this describes your situation, you should seek advice from your doctor as a matter of urgency. Don't wait until you are completely exhausted or events reach a crisis point before asking for help. Many people find it hard to ask for help because they feel this is a sign of failure or means they are abandoning the person that they are caring for. It isn't, and you aren't. Caring is a difficult business and by seeking help, you are actually increasing the chance that you can cope in the long term, so helping ensure your welfare and that of the person you are caring for.

Treatments may include antidepressants, counselling or other psychological treatments. Looking after yourself and ensuring that you take regular exercise and relaxation are also important factors in dealing with depression. A carer's assessment (or a review if you have already had one) would also help you to identify the contributory factors involved and what services could be put in place to help you cope in the future.

Spirituality

Being diagnosed with a chronic health condition or caring for someone with one can have a profound effect on your spirituality.

Spirituality can be defined in many ways. For some people it is a religious faith or culture that defines who they are, everything they do in life, and their attitudes and feelings. This may include attitudes to disability that may be positive or negative. For others, it is more about their sense of self and the things that matter to them or their outlook on life. This is very individual and may include what they do for a living, their family, the music they like or the football team they support, creative activities, their garden and so on.

Some people find the effects on their spirituality are positive. Having an illness/disability, or caring for someone with one, enriches their spiritual life and makes them realize what aspects of their life are really important to them. Any religious or spiritual experience they already have may become deeper and lead them to explore issues that they had never previously considered.

For others, the consequences are more unsettling and may lead to a spiritual crisis. If they have a religious faith, they may feel abandoned by the God from whom they previously obtained a lot of comfort and strength. People who are not religious may find that ill health or caring responsibilities threaten something that made up a large part of their sense of self, such as a chosen career from which they derived enormous satisfaction. Finding new activities to compensate can be an important way of coping with their loss.

Because spirituality is so individual, there are no simple answers to managing the impact that caring may have on yours. Finding someone to talk to about how you are feeling may be the first step, perhaps a friend or family member or through your place of worship, a chaplain at your local hospital (who will usually talk to anyone who needs someone to talk to, regardless of their spiritual background) or a professional counsellor.

The Royal College of Psychiatrists has a leaflet, 'Spirituality and Mental Health', which explores this issue in more depth.

If the person you are caring for has a terminal or life-limiting condition, the local hospice may be able to provide spiritual support. The approach is usually holistic and in addition to medical and nursing care, services might include counselling, complementary therapies, spiritual care, art, music, physiotherapy, reminiscence, beauty treatments and bereavement support. Further information can be obtained from Help the Hospices.

You may have a religious faith or culture that influences your attitude towards certain medical treatments, procedures, or dietary factors (e.g. if the person you are caring for has to go into hospital or for respite care). Don't be afraid to discuss these with the health or social care professionals involved in the care of the person you are caring for, so that suitable arrangements can be made to respect your beliefs.

Looking after yourself

All too often, carers' time and energies are so focused on the person they are caring for, that they neglect their own needs. Remember that your health is just as important, so don't neglect it. Make sure you eat properly and exercise regularly. Relaxation techniques such as yoga, meditation, aromatherapy and reflexology can also help.

Looking after yourself also involves making sure you don't try to do too much. Set priorities and, if the tasks you have are overwhelming, ask for help. Sometimes, breaking up large difficulties into smaller, more manageable pieces can help. Make sure that you have time for yourself away from caring to pursue your own interests. Accept help from other people and don't feel guilty about your feelings or your need to have a life of your own away from caring.

Personal experiences

Anne

Anne found juggling everything and adjusting to the life-limiting nature of her daughter, Anna's, condition very difficult. 'You had to say to yourself well I'm investing in the living here and to some extent you had to shut out the fact that it came with a time limit. There were times when I railed against the relentlessness of caring but I had no choice but to keep going. Sometimes I used to get so frustrated and angry but at the same time, if someone had said, "Okay we'll take her away, give you someone else's child", I'd have said on your bike. I remember one Christmas, I had got myself into such a state and felt I couldn't take any more and then something happened to make it shift and lift the cloud.'

She also says that there was a feeling of failure that 'You have not managed to do it yourself and you have had to get help. I remember too when I was expecting Robert, several people said we would have to have more respite – and I burst into tears because I had said up to then that "Anna goes out of this house over my dead body." It wasn't so much about me being indispensable but me having failed because I had to have help. Sometimes, I found it easier to accept the need for support if I could see it as something positive to help Anna. For instance, when Anna was at school she had two overnights a week during term-time. We called it respite, but they said it was to progress Anna's social and personal development because they felt, and they were right, that I couldn't manage all three children.'

One of the main supports to Anne while she was caring was the paediatric community sister. 'She was a lifeline,' Anne says, 'She would sometimes visit twice in a day – if in the morning she saw that I was struggling to cope with Anna's medication, tube-feeding or suction, she would pitch up in the afternoon or early evening with the excuse that she had forgotten something, but I knew she hadn't. I couldn't have done it all without her.'

Hugh

Hugh Marriott is the author of *The Selfish Pig's Guide to Caring*, one of the few books on caring I could find written by a carer. Hugh has been caring for several years for his wife, Cathie, who has Huntington's disease, a long-term hereditary neurological condition that causes gradual physical, mental and emotional changes.

Around the time symptoms of Huntington's disease began to impact on their lives, Hugh and Cathie sold their house, bought a sailing boat and embarked on what was to become a nine-year voyage of discovery. By the time Cathie could no longer get in or out of their small dingy or safely clamber on board their boat, they had visited 40 countries and sailed almost the whole way around the world.

After moving ashore again, Hugh settled down to write about the most significant aspect of the voyage: coming to terms with caring for someone who has a debilitating disease. In his book, he tries to put his finger on the advice he would like to have been given while he was struggling to learn new skills and find his way in an unfamiliar role.

What is refreshing about his book is that he is not afraid to explore, in a brutally frank, but often amusing way, the mixed feelings that carers often have about their situation, including those they may find difficult to admit to others, such as 'thoughts of murder'. He also talks about subjects that are often difficult for carers to discuss with healthcare professionals, such as sex, continence and dealing with inappropriate and hurtful responses from people who fail to understand a carer's situation.

At the start of the book, he explains that his book is for carers 'who have come reluctantly to caring. We feel bad about our unwillingness, and secretly think of ourselves as selfish pigs. Like pigs in nature, we can be of either sex. Also like real pigs, we are not necessarily, or at least always, disagreeable and unpleasant. But we're certainly obstinate.'

Sue

Sue, who cared for her father for many years, recently read Hugh's book at an emotionally difficult time when she was helping care for an aunt with cancer. She says, 'Keeping your sanity as a carer is important. I recognized much of what he said from my experiences with my father and my aunt. I found his candid approach refreshing and reassuring, especially in admitting to the difficult feelings and frustrations that he has while wanting to care for his wife. I also liked the fact that he wasn't afraid to discuss the embarrassing aspects you often have to face.'

8

Respite care and holidays

If you are to maintain your own health and cope with your responsibilities, you need regular breaks from caring. This is often called
respite care. The aim is to provide temporary caring arrangements so
that carers can have a rest and recharge their batteries. How carers use
the time is up to them – shopping, enjoying sports or leisure pursuits,
meeting friends or simply relaxing.

Respite care can take many forms. It might involve a few hours
every week, or less frequent but longer periods of time. Care may be
provided:

- outside the home, for example, at a day centre or residential facility
  such as a care home;
- in the form of a holiday. This may involve the person being cared
  for going away on his or her own or with the carer. In the latter case,
  care will be provided by other people so the carer gets a rest;
- within the person's home.

Your local social services department, health authority, voluntary
organizations or private establishments may all provide respite care.

Because so much depends on your particular needs and your local
area, the first step is to contact your local social services department
to explore the options available and to arrange for an assessment to
determine your needs and those of the person you are caring for. See
Chapter 4: Community care.

The Princess Royal Trust for Carers centres and Carers UK can also
provide you with information about respite care. See Chapter 2: Sources
of information and advice.

Other good sources of information on respite care are voluntary
organizations that support people with a particular health condition.
They will understand your particular needs and may be able to point
you to relevant services. Some of these provide holiday/respite care
services themselves or produce guides and campaign for better provision. Examples include:

- The Parkinson's Disease Society's annual *Holidays and Respite Care
  Guide*.[25]

- Mencap developed a 'short breaks charter' in 2006 and is campaigning for good short breaks for people with a learning disability and their families/carer. Their helpline can provide information on respite care for children with learning difficulties.
- Arthritis Care has four seaside hotels that offer breaks to people with arthritis, their families and friends.

There are also some organizations that specialize in providing respite care/holiday services and/or information for people with disabilities and their carers. For example:

Break provides residential and day care services for children, adults and families with special needs, including holidays and respite care. Services include homes for children, family assessments and day care for adults with learning difficulties, respite care, specialist childcare and UK holidays in Norfolk and the West Country.

Tourism for All aims to help disabled and older people lead independent lives by enhancing their ability to travel. They provide information on transport, accommodation, visitor attractions, activity holidays and respite care establishments in the UK and overseas.

Shared Care Network is a national organization that promotes family-based short breaks for disabled children in England, Wales and Northern Ireland. It represents over 300 local schemes that link disabled children with people in the community providing regular short-term care.

Vitalise (formerly known as Winged Fellowship Trust) provides breaks for disabled adults, children and their carers at five accessible UK centres in Cornwall, Nottingham, Southport, Essex and Southampton. Vitalise also publishes guides to other breaks and holidays in the UK and Europe.

Care at home

Some agencies and voluntary organizations provide professional carers to help people in their own home. Your local social services department or carers' organization should be able to advise further on what is available in your area.

The British Nursing Association is one such agency, which provides professional carers of differing levels of qualification – home helps, care assistants, nurses. The services they offer include convalescent care, night care, personal care, shopping, companionship and respite care.[26] See <www.bna.co.uk> for more information.

Crossroads – Caring for Carers aims to improve the lives of carers by giving them time to have a break and be themselves. Their schemes, available in most parts of England and Wales, offer a range of services to meet local needs, and many include additional services such as young carers' projects, holiday play schemes for disabled children and care for people who are terminally ill. (See an example of one scheme at the end of this chapter.)

The UK Home Care Association (UKHCA) is the professional association of home care providers from the independent, voluntary, not-for-profit and statutory sectors. UKHCA members agree to abide by the association's code of practice. They have a section on choosing care on their website <www.ukhca.org.uk>.

Funding for respite care and holidays

Whether you will have to pay for respite care will depend on your local social services department's charging policy – these are usually means-tested. A financial assessment is usually done by social services with the carer's assessment to ascertain whether you will be charged for any services they provide. Funding is also sometimes available from voluntary organizations or trusts if you meet their criteria. The organizations mentioned earlier in this chapter can advise further. See Chapter 4: Community care and Chapter 5: Finances.

Accepting the need for respite care

Some carers find it hard to accept their need for respite care. They feel guilty at needing a break and time to themselves. If you feel like this, remember that respite care enables you to rest and look after your own health. Your ability to carry on caring can be compromised if you never take a break. The Princess Royal Trust for Carers website suggests that you remember: 'In most jobs you get paid holidays – you should try to take some time off from caring too!'[27]

Many carers worry that no one can provide the level of care that they give. While nobody can provide the degree of love and attention that your caring, combined with the extra things that your relationship with him or her includes, satisfactory respite care is still possible. It is just a matter of finding something that suits you and the person you are caring for.

Sometimes the person being cared for is resistant, or frightened by the need for the carer to have a break. Wherever possible, involve him or her in all decisions about respite care. See if a trial period can be arranged. Even though the principal purpose of respite care is to give the carer a break, the right respite care can also benefit the person being cared for by providing a change, opportunities to learn new things or pursue existing interests, have therapy and meet other people.

You may also find it helpful to talk to other carers about their experiences of respite care. See Chapter 7: Emotional, psychological and spiritual impact.

Planning for emergencies

Many carers worry about what would happen to the person they are caring for if they were unwell or had an accident. Preparing in advance will minimize the disruption and worry that such a situation might cause. Your local social services department should be able to help you to put an emergency plan together.

Carers UK publishes some useful tips for planning for an emergency on their website.[28] Some of the following information is based on this.

Carers' emergency schemes: Some local authorities and carers' centres in England run these. An emergency plan is drawn up and held by the scheme, which provides a 24-hour response service. Carers carry a card with the scheme's telephone number and a unique PIN number (to avoid any personal details appearing on the card). If there is an emergency, the carer or someone else can call the scheme, which will activate the plan. The plan might simply be a list of friends or family who can help or professional help. It would include individual requirements, such as medication. For more information on those currently available and other emergency help schemes available in your area, contact your local social services department. Carers UK and the Princess Royal Trust for Carers can also advise.

Community alarms: Many local authorities, as well as voluntary organizations such as Age Concern and Help the Aged, run community alarm schemes. In the event of an accident, the person can push a button on the phone or a device worn around the wrist or neck to summon help from a 24-hour response centre. A fee is charged for most of these systems but there are usually exemptions for some people on low incomes. Your social services department should be able to advise you.

Relatives and friends: If relatives or friends will provide care in an emergency, discuss in advance what they will need to do. Prepare some notes in a folder, kept in a known, accessible place. These should include:

- contact details – for family and healthcare professionals, voluntary organizations and anyone involved in the care of the person;
- medication – what is taken, how it is taken and when;
- the care the person needs;
- a checklist of how to cope with particular situations or concerns that the person being cared for can experience, e.g. what to do if the person has a fall;
- information about the person's preferences and anything else you think it is important for emergency carers to know;
- information about any health condition.

Carers' emergency cards: It can be very important to carry something in your purse, wallet or programmed in your mobile that identifies you as a carer and includes the contact details of people to contact in an emergency. A carers' emergency card like this is available from Carers UK.

Travelling abroad[29]

Many carers travel abroad with the person they are caring for. Planning carefully before you go to take account of any potential difficulties is the secret to ensuring a successful trip. Particular concerns can include flying and travelling with medication.

Book with the airline well in advance of your travel date and make sure you tell them about any special assistance you may require. Assistance can also be arranged in advance at airports. The airline or your travel agent should be able to advise you further about this. The term used is 'assisted travel'.

It is very important to take a letter from the doctor that states that the person you are caring for is fit to travel, detailing any medication and the health condition it treats. This will help you if there are any queries at customs or you run into any difficulties while you are abroad.

You should be able to take as much prescription medicines as you need, provided it does not contain any controlled drugs, i.e. drugs that can only be prescribed under the guidelines of the Misuse of Drugs Act (1971) and Regulations (1973, 1985), usually drugs that have the potential for dependence or abuse. Some prescription medicines contain controlled drugs and if they do, there are limits on the amount that you can take with you. HM Revenue and Customs (the new government department which is now responsible for the business of the former Inland Revenue and HM Customs) publish a guide to taking medicines abroad (Public Notice 4). If you have any doubts about whether any drugs you are taking contain controlled drugs, check with your doctor or HM Revenue and Customs.

You should also note that some countries require you to obtain an import permit to bring in some types of prescribed drugs for personal use. You should check what is required with the embassy of the country you are visiting. Make sure that you take extra supplies of the medication with you just in case it is not available in the country you are visiting.

It is recommended that you carry any medication in your hand luggage. However, because of the increased incidences of terrorism around the world, security at airports and on airplanes is much tighter these days, and is sometimes subject to change at short notice. Therefore, you should contact the airline you are travelling with well in advance of your travel date to ascertain what you will be able to take with you in hand luggage and what documentation you will require to explain what you have and why. For example, if you will be carrying any syringes, you must have a doctor's note to explain why you have them. If the airline has banned passengers from carrying any sharp objects or medication in hand luggage, ask them what arrangements you can make if you need access to them on the flight.

Check what the health service arrangements are for the country you are visiting. The travel advice section of the Department of Health's website, <www.dh.gov.uk>, can provide more information.

You should also ensure that you have adequate insurance to cover any medical emergencies you might encounter while you are away. If travelling to a European Union (EU) country, take European Health Insurance (EHIC) cards with you. These can be obtained from your local post office.

Personal experiences

Sonia and her husband, Tom, have some respite support from Crossroads – Caring for Carers. 'They are brilliant and take John, our son with learning disabilities, out in the summer.' They also have direct payments (see Chapter 5: Finances) for three hours a week. 'Tom and I like to go to the theatre so we use the direct payments to pay for someone to look after John and his brother, Sam. It's lovely because the children like it and we like it. However, finding the right respite care workers has been very difficult. In the end I found two people through word of mouth from other parents, who both work at one of the local special schools. I feel quite confident about leaving them, which is important. I don't use the three hours religiously every week but sometimes build it up so we can go away overnight. I do feel there is always a pressure to find people who are cheap to pay but that isn't possible when you need a high level of skills. There is only one level of payment for direct payments and I don't think that is right because different children have different levels of care.'

When *Anne* was caring for her daughter Anna, the respite facilities available to the family varied. 'For a while she went to stay with a family every six weeks for an overnight or weekend stay as part of the Share a Care scheme but this stopped because social services reorganized and for a while we had nothing. Then as she moved through school (a unit for the multidisabled visually impaired at the Royal Blind School in Edinburgh), we got a lot of support from them. The children's hospice was also very good. A less positive experience of respite care was when she went into adult services at the age of 16. She had oxygen requirements and health needs, and no suitable adult respite service was available other than a nursing home for severely disabled complex needs adults. Poor Anna at the age 16 was in with these adults in their 40s and 50s who had significantly additional needs.'

May Darke runs a local Crossroads – Caring for Carers scheme in Brentwood, Essex. Their services cater for any kind of disability and referrals are taken from anyone in the area including the carers themselves, GPs, health and social services, and voluntary organizations. 'The aim of Crossroads,' May says, 'is to support the carers in their caring role. Helping them to continue caring and keep the person being cared for at home.'

Because their resources are limited, most of the breaks Brentwood Crossroads provide are of up to four hours' duration a week in the person's home, as well as occasional extra respite care for special occasions – for instance if the carer wants to attend a wedding.

'The unique thing about Crossroads is the fact that once we allocate a support worker, they will see that same person every week. They often become friends with them and keep in contact with carers even when they stop caring,' May explains. Depending on individual needs, the support worker may do activities with the person being cared for or simply talk to them. Whether carers pay for the service or not depends on their financial situation – for instance, whether they are in receipt of direct payments; however, service is not denied to carers because they can't afford it.

The service also supports carers when they stop caring, perhaps because the person being cared for has died or gone to live in residential care. May says, 'Stopping caring is a very difficult time for many carers because all the services that they have had stop. All these people who were coming in during the day are suddenly not there any more and the carer doesn't know what to do sometimes. Our support workers will continue to visit them for some weeks after they stop caring to provide some emotional support at this difficult time.'

9

Caring for children

Around 770,000 children (seven per cent) in the UK are disabled and 14 per cent of the country's carers look after a disabled child. This population has changed significantly in the past two decades because of increases in autism spectrum conditions and the fact that more babies and children are surviving, living longer and with more complex needs, because of medical and technological advances.

Caring for a disabled child is a very challenging experience – practically, financially and emotionally. However, these children are usually much loved and many carers find it rewarding to watch them develop.

This chapter discusses some of the key factors that may be involved in caring for a disabled child, concentrating specifically on the needs of their parents. It highlights some of the main sources, including Contact a Family, a leading UK voluntary organization supporting families of disabled children, whose resources I have used extensively as reference materials.

Diagnosis

The time of diagnosis of a child's disability usually has an enormous psychological, emotional and spiritual impact on parents. The manner in which it is imparted and the support mechanisms that are available are crucial factors in helping them to cope at this stage.

Ruth, who cares for her daughter and works as a volunteer local parent rep for Contact a Family says, 'Sometimes it takes a long time to get a diagnosis and some people never receive one. Some people can live with this uncertainty but others find it very hard because they want the specifics. Although many aspects of caring for a disabled child are similar, no matter what the condition they have is, a lot of things depend on having a diagnosis. You can often get more services if you have one and filling in benefit forms and being successful in your application can be more difficult if you don't have a diagnosis.'

Many parents say that talking to other carers who are in a similar position is the greatest support at the point of diagnosis. One carer I met at a Mencap carers' support group described how when she was in despair, another carer had helped her to accept her situation and enabled her to believe she would be able to cope with her daughter's learning disability. Obtaining the information that will help you make sense of your position is also vital.

Being a parent and a carer

For carers of disabled children, separating out their caring role from their family roles can be difficult – most I spoke to saw themselves first and foremost as parents.

Ruth says, 'Many do find it hard to separate out the role of carer from being a parent – it's very entwined. Some people think that you use the term when you are caring for someone who is elderly. Others identify "carers" with someone who is paid. I think they often think caring is part of their responsibility of being a parent and don't realize the added aspects that come with it.'

Eva, who has been caring for her daughter for 20 years, sees herself as a parent and a carer. 'Yes, I'm her parent, but I also have to do things for her that you normally wouldn't do and it is important to separate the two.' She says the dual role can be more difficult for the person being cared for than the carer. 'I think sometimes she prefers to have her personal care done by other people. She doesn't mind me doing it but it chips even more away from her independence if I do. Sometimes she has tried to protect us by not complaining about things she should have done because she thought it would upset us.'

Services

A variety of services to help you care for your disabled child should be available through health and social services. Up to the age of 18 a disabled child's needs are assessed under the Children Act 1989. From the age of 18 there is a transfer to adult services under the NHS and Community Care Act. What is available will depend on provision in your local area. Some carers have found accessing these services difficult and many say that you have to keep 'banging on the door' to be successful. However, some also said they had a great deal of support from their local services. See Chapter 3: Healthcare professionals and Chapter 4: Community care.

Education

The education of a disabled child is a vital aspect of their life. This is usually arranged through your Local Education Authority (LEA). You need to ensure that you find out as much as possible about the options available to your child so that they enjoy their time at school and their potential is developed to the full. It goes without saying that this is a complicated subject on which you need expert advice.

Legally, 'special needs education' refers to children who 'all have learning difficulties or disabilities that make it harder for them to learn than most children of the same age. These children may need extra or different help from that given to other children of the same age.'[30] Anyone requiring this kind of assistance is provided with a statement of their special education needs, which sets out their needs and the help they should have. This is reviewed annually to ensure that any extra support given continues to meet their needs.[31]

The government's website for teachers includes a section on special educational needs and disability, which has information for parents and carers, such as the booklet, 'Special Education Needs: A guide for parents and carers'. This makes the following basic points:

- All children with special educational needs should have their needs met.
- The special educational needs of children are normally met in mainstream (ordinary) early education settings or schools.
- Your views should be taken into account and the wishes of your child should be listened to.
- You have a vital role in supporting your child's education and you should be consulted about all the decisions that affect your child.
- Children with special educational needs should get a broad, well-balanced and relevant education, including the foundation stage curriculum (for children aged 3–5) or the National Curriculum (for children aged 5–16).

See <www.teachernet.gov.uk/wholeschool/sen/>.

Contact a Family publishes a pack, *Disabled Education and Disability: A parents' guide to rights from nursery to university*.[32] For Scotland, where the system is different, they have a fact sheet, 'Additional Support for Learning'.[33] Voluntary organizations concerned with disabled children should also be able to advise further.

Finances

Having a disabled child has a huge impact on the finances of many families. It costs up to three times as much to raise a disabled child as it does to raise one without disabilities. The income of families with disabled children averages £15,270, which is 23.5 per cent below the UK mean income of £19,968, and 21.8 per cent have incomes that are less than half this. Only 16 per cent of mothers with disabled children work, compared to 61 per cent of other mothers. The costs of caring are often greater – for instance, childcare costs around £5.50 per hour for a disabled child, compared to around £3.50 for other children. Debt can be a major issue for many families.[34]

Financial benefits and services are available to help you cope with the costs of caring for your disabled child and it is extremely important that you check what financial benefits you are entitled to. The health and social care professionals involved in your care won't necessarily advise you on this. See the Contact a Family fact sheet: 'Benefits, Tax Credits and Other Financial Help' for more information.

See also Chapter 5: Finances and Chapter 6: Employment and education for carers.

Family relationships

Caring for a disabled child can cause considerable relationship problems and family tensions. One study found that 31 per cent of couples report some problems, 13 per cent cite major problems and 9 per cent actually separate. One carer I spoke to said that there was considerable tension between her and her husband because they had different attitudes towards the caring situation that they found themselves in. 'My husband said that we should do everything for our child because she is never going to be different, whereas I wanted to try and give her some life skills for self-esteem and quality of life.'

Tensions can also exist between other members of the family. The availability of respite care is an important ingredient in lessening family relationship stress. Obtaining support to help you with any particular problems is also important. Don't let problems fester until they reach crisis point. Some of the organizations mentioned at the end of this chapter should be able to advise or refer you to sources of further help.

Transition between childhood and adulthood

Adolescence is an emotionally and psychologically challenging time for any parent but for those with disabled/ill children there are additional concerns because decisions have to be made about the future. A transition plan (previously called a 'future needs assessment' in Scotland but subject to change as a result of the new Additional Support for Learning Act being enforced) will usually be drawn up, by the local education authority, in the school year 9 (the year in which young people turn 14), and will be concerned with ongoing school and post-school provision. Your financial situation can also change after 16 – children may be able to claim benefits in their own right but this can affect benefits you may be receiving for them.

People I spoke to stressed the importance of starting the planning of this as early as possible. Many felt that less support was available under Adult Services than Children's Services, which could cause problems, especially if you were not prepared.

Contact a Family publish guides to this stage, *Transition: England and Wales* and *Post 16 Transition* in Scotland (under review to take account of legislative changes). For information about Northern Ireland, contact their national office.

The Family Fund has a website for young people, parents and carers which discusses the opportunities available to young people who are disabled once they reach 16. See <www.after16.org.uk>.

Some voluntary organizations, such as Mencap, offer support and advice on issues relating to this stage in a disabled person's life.

Care after the parent dies

Another major concern is ensuring the child's financial security and welfare after parents die. Careful planning and expert advice is extremely important. This is discussed further in Chapter 5: Finances.

Sources of further help and advice

Contact a Family provides advice, information and support to families with disabled children across the UK. Its national freephone helpline, publications and comprehensive website provide help on all aspects of bringing up a disabled child.

Local area volunteer representatives (who are themselves parents of children with disabilities), national offices in Scotland, Wales and

Northern Ireland, English regional offices and London projects provide specialist local support. The offices also run workshops and events for parents and families. In some parts of the UK, its Family Support Service provides short-term help for families, to help them over a crisis or to resolve a particular issue.

Wherever possible, Contact a Family puts parents in touch with others in a similar position, either through condition-specific support groups or by helping parents set up new support groups. For children with very rare conditions, the organization can link families on a one to one basis through the helpline or their dedicated website – see <www.makingcontact.org>. The organization also publishes an annual *Directory of Specific Conditions, Rare Disorders and UK Family Support Groups*.

Contact a Family also works increasingly with parents and professionals to develop consultation and participation programmes, which help ensure that local services (health, social care and education) are designed to meet local needs. Campaigning to improve the circumstances of families of disabled children is also an important part of its work.

There are many voluntary organizations dealing with specific health conditions that affect children that can provide you with detailed information and support to help you to cope with the specifics of the disorder that you are dealing with. Some examples include:

- ASBAH – spina bifida and hydrocephalus;
- RNIB – visual impairments (in children and adults);
- CLIC Sargent – for children with cancer;
- Mencap (Enable in Scotland) – learning difficulties;
- National Deaf Children's Society – hearing;
- Scope – cerebral palsy;
- National Autistic Society – autism.

Charities that focus on the needs of children in general, such as Barnardo's, the Children's Society and NCH, the children's charity, also support disabled children and their families. See Chapter 2: Sources of information and advice.

One Parent Families is a voluntary organization that supports lone parents through practical advice and information as well as campaigning on key issues that affect them. This includes a specialist advice service for lone parents who are caring for a child who has a disability or long-term health problem, which is available through their helpline, and publications such as 'The Lone Parent Guide to Caring for a Child with Additional Needs'. There is also an online forum where you can share ideas and experiences with other lone parent carers.

Whizz-Kidz is a registered charity that helps disabled children to move around independently by providing customized wheelchairs, tricycles and other specialized mobility equipment as well as wheelchair training, information and advice. Their website includes a 'Kidz Zone' for disabled children, which includes personal stories.

Every Child Matters: Change for Children is a government initiative to promote the well-being of children and young people from birth to the age of 19. It aims for every child, whatever their background or circumstances, to have the support they need to be healthy, stay safe, enjoy and achieve, make a positive contribution and achieve economic well-being. See <www.ecm.gov.uk>. This has led to Every Disabled Child Matters, a campaign, involving several children's voluntary organizations, to get rights and justice for every disabled child. See <www.edcm.org.uk> for more information.

Caring for a Disabled Child by Abigail Knight, which I have used as a resource while writing this chapter, provides a concise, practical guide to many of the issues discussed here.

Personal experiences

Ruth

Ruth lives with her husband, a teacher, and their two children, Alice, nine, who has severe learning difficulties and limited mobility, and David, seven.

Ruth's caring responsibilities are extensive and include providing personal care tasks such as dressing, washing, continence care and administering medication. Recently Alice has learnt to walk with splints but because she has no idea of safety, Ruth has to be there to check the paths are clear, etc. Alice has some verbal communication and uses a lot of non-verbal communication such as pointing, but Ruth often has to help interpret what she is saying to other people. Ruth also often finds herself explaining Alice's fairly extensive birthmark to people they meet. She says, 'I think it is quite nice when people ask, but dealing with the staring is hard.'

'Quite often,' Ruth adds, 'the difficulties are not with caring but with the services that surround that and co-ordinating them. I need to be proactive because nobody reminds you when you are due a review. The constant fighting for services and keeping the momentum going is the hardest aspect of caring for me – nobody could have told me how much fighting I would have to do. It's things like constantly having to prove you need services and fill in forms. For instance, why do we have to fill in Disability Living Allowance forms so frequently when we have a child with a diagnosis and a prognosis? It worries me because of all the vulnerable families that are out there who can't do it for themselves – and they probably need it the most.'

Before she had her family, Ruth worked as a children's nurse and health visitor, but doesn't feel able to do paid work at the moment. 'Although my daughter is quite stable, she still has a lot of hospital appointments. I just feel I couldn't be in work because I would be off a lot of the time and I don't think it would be fair.' However, for the past couple of years she has been a volunteer parent rep for Contact a Family. This involves disseminating the organization's information to families of disabled children and the professionals who work with them – through one-to-one, telephone or email contact or by attending information days. 'I feel it gives me a purpose and I get a lot of satisfaction from feeling that I am hopefully making a difference. I have found lately that email often seems to be a preferred way for people to make contact. Some parents don't phone because they find it too hard to make the call, so I try to go to places and things where I may meet parents. Sometimes seeing me and talking to me reassures them enough to make contact.'

The questions Ruth is asked by parents vary, but they often want information about specific conditions. 'They are often looking for specifics that I can't always help them with. However, I can usually signpost them to other sources of information and support.'

Key workers and adequate respite care are two aspects that Ruth feels have had an impact on how she cares. Key workers or lead professionals means the family having one key worker that they contact to sort out any problems they have, rather than having numerous ones that they have to keep coordinating. When local services use this approach to providing care, it can make a great deal of positive difference to a carer's life. Where it isn't in place, many carers find that there isn't much communication between professionals and they often find themselves repeating the same information over and over again.

'Respite care should be given regularly, especially for families whose children don't sleep. Often carers don't get much respite – things build up and up and then it is needed urgently. Often, it could have been given in a way that meant the family didn't get into a crisis state and would ultimately reduce the amount of money that was used to fund the service.'

For Ruth, the positive side of caring has been the whole new range of friends she has made and the support of existing friends. She says, 'I have a completely different way of living now than I did before but it's not all negative. I think I am a much stronger person for having Alice and my priorities have changed for the better.'

Anne

Anne cared for her daughter Anna for 17 years, from birth until her death in 2001. Anna was diagnosed with a relatively rare chromosome disorder called Cri du Chat syndrome. Her symptoms were severe because an additional chromosome was implicated and her condition was life-limiting because of a heart disorder.

Anne says getting Anna's diagnosis was a traumatic experience. 'It was one of these long, drawn-out situations. There was a lot of delaying and prevaricating on the part of the medics. They obviously knew what she had, but delayed telling us first so the genetic kariotyping could be performed and then by saying the tests had been mislaid. In the end we had to pin them up against a wall to get the truth out of them. It is so frustrating when you know you are being messed around and all you want is a straight answer so you know what you are dealing with.'

Anne now works for Contact a Family in Scotland as Paediatric Project Officer. 'In my job I now advocate for there to be two professionals present when the diagnosis is made – one giving it and the other observing. Also for the parents to be supported, to have something written to take away and a contact person to go back to. Why is that so hard to arrange?'

Anne's caring role was extensive because Anna was unable to do anything for herself, and was shared with her husband, Stewart, daughter Joan, son Robert and other members of the family. Anne says, 'The grandmothers were fantastic, particularly my husband's mother who was my "right-hand woman" and who has suffered a lot from losing Anna because she had a relationship with her that went well beyond being a grandparent.'

The lack of resources, non-delivery and lack of coordination of health and social care services were the hardest aspects of caring for Anne. 'I had to keep beating on the door. I felt I had to oversee everything because if I took my eye off the ball, it would suddenly go. Goodness knows what you do if you are not in a position to do this.'

The impact of her caring role on finances was also very hard. 'My career as a teacher just completely foundered. I was able to keep working but almost at a cost to myself. I did supply teaching but ended up paying more out in childcare some weeks. Getting "fit for purpose" childcare was also a major problem.'

Because Anna had a visual impairment, the family decided that a
unit for the multidisabled at the local blind school was the best place
for her education. 'It had a very high student–teacher ratio which
meant she had individual attention.'

From caring for Anna, Anne feels she gained a great deal of knowledge and skills that she now uses in her work for Contact a Family. 'I
wouldn't have the job without that knowledge,' she says. 'I have met
some fabulous people who I might never have encountered otherwise.
I feel I have developed greater compassion and understanding of others
as well.'

Jacqui

Jacqui Jackson is the single mother of seven children, four of whom
have learning disabilities. She has written a book, *Multicoloured Mayhem:
Parenting the many shades of adolescents and children with autism, Asperger
syndrome and AD/HD*, in which she shares her experiences of parenting
young people with such a wide range of conditions. The book provides
factual information on the conditions her children have and a great
deal of practical advice on issues such as family and sibling relationships, adolescence, holidays (coping with change), safety and surviving
as a parent. Her son, Luke, has written a book on his condition, *Freaks,
Geeks and Asperger Syndrome*, and the Jackson family's life has been the
subject of a recent TV documentary.

10

Caring at a distance

As well as the many carers who live with the person they are caring for, a considerable number care for relatives or friends at a distance. These are often elderly people who are living in their own home but need support to stay there and maintain a good quality of life.

Despite the fact that people who care at distance often don't identify themselves as carers, their lives can be greatly affected by the responsibilities they have, in terms of the time involved, the drain on financial resources and the emotional impact.

Caring for someone at a distance can be a very frustrating experience, especially if the person being cared for is very independent and reluctant to accept help. The existing relationship that you have with them will be a significant and complicating factor – for instance, a parent may find it difficult to accept that their child now takes care of them. *Sue*, who cared for her father, says, 'I found that continual negotiation was necessary in order to strike a happy medium between ensuring that my father received the support he needed and allowing him to retain control over his life.'

Ascertaining correctly what the situation is at a distance can also be difficult. *Michael*, whose 90-year-old father lives 240 miles away from him, says, 'Without face-to-face contact, how do you determine whether what is being said is a normal state of affairs or an emergency?' This state of affairs can be compounded if the person being cared for is reluctant to reveal the true situation, uses denial as a coping mechanism or becomes emotionally demanding out of fear, confusion or ill health.

Finding, vetting and coordinating services to help your relative can be problematic when you don't live in the local area and have limited time to visit. Sometimes, additional support can be provided by relatives/neighbours but where this is not possible, you are very reliant on what statutory health and social services are available locally. These can be very good, but finding them can take a lot of time, effort and endless battling.

Juggling caring responsibilities with other demands on your life can have enormous impact when you are caring at a distance – especially with the hanging uncertainty about when you might be called to deal with an emergency. Another huge concern is getting an employer to understand your needs as a carer so that they provide family-friendly policies that are flexible enough to give you time off to help your relative when you need to. This issue is discussed in Chapter 6: Employment and education for carers.

Sources of information

There are not always easy answers to the issues that may confront you when caring at a distance. However, a community care assessment for the person you are caring for and a carer's assessment for you would help you to identify areas of need and services that might be available to help you both. (See Chapter 4: Community care.)

The local social services, GP surgery, Citizens Advice and carers' organizations/centres should be able to provide you with further information on what is available in the area where your relative/friend lives.

Branches of voluntary organizations relevant to your relative's situation can be good sources of information, support and social contact. Contact with other carers in a similar position can provide much-needed emotional support and opportunities to share ideas and tips – in person, on the telephone or through online forums. See Chapter 7: Emotional, psychological and spiritual impact.

Age Concern publishes *Caring for Someone at a Distance* by Julie Spencer-Cingöz. Help the Aged has an information sheet called 'Living Alone Safely' which includes information on issues that affect older people who live on their own.

If you are worried about how the person you are caring for at a distance would summon help if they had a fall or accident, a community alarm system might be a solution. See Chapter 4: Community care.

Personal experiences

Michael

Michael lives in southern England with his family. His elderly father has lived alone 240 miles away since Michael's mother, who had several health problems, died three years ago.

Although Michael's father manages by himself on a day-to-day basis, his health is affected by Crohn's disease and difficulties with swallowing. As his father's only living close relative, Michael's caring role mainly involves helping his father to maintain his independence and dignity, providing emotional support and ensuring that he has the support around him that he needs and deserves. Although this responsibility is difficult at times, Michael has 'over time become more willing to consider that I have a duty and a role as a "carer" to assist and intervene'.

He has found contact difficult when his father is ill. He says, 'There are lots of gadgets, gismos and clever telephones that help people living on their own. However, most seem to be readily disabled by leaving a phone off the hook. My father is extremely technically literate and loves gadgets, but when he is ill and bedridden it is impossible to get him to answer the phone. This can be worrying because suddenly everything relies on knowing the neighbours and getting them to pop round. The MSN messenger service on his computer has proved a handy way of checking that he is okay. I know he switches it on at certain times in the day so if I don't see his contact details come up, I know he isn't well, even when he doesn't admit it to me on the phone.'

Michael does not see himself as a carer because of the distance separating them and says his immensely independent father 'would certainly be insulted if I claimed I was. However, I do feel I have to do all I can and from my experiences of helping both my father and mother over the past ten years, have come to realize what a challenge this is – one that is only likely to get harder.'

For Michael, the hardest part about caring has been the realization that 'this is a long-term role with no end and that I am dependent on strangers to do the most important things for my loved ones. Sometimes I have felt completely unable to help through lack of knowledge and contact. Seemingly trivial things like finding a cleaner have seemed a major challenge, especially remotely. Bizarrely, given that we live in the Internet age, finding advice has been very, very difficult.

'Being reliant on health and social care professionals who have little ability to build a personal relationship with him is tough. In my experience, social services seem completely disjointed and point to a network of associations, quangos, self-help groups and bodies – many of which seem to specialize in signposting you to other organizations, providing leaflets but not actually doing any caring. This is particularly hard when you don't live in the same area. My father only got benefits because he ran into a neighbour who worked for the local Citizens Advice bureau and convinced him she could help him fill in the forms. This random act of kindness has transformed his life and was something that I – a professional, educated person – had been unable to achieve.

'Now we have some local support from nurses aligned to his GP who are known and have been able to suggest assistance and build up trust. This situation was arranged through direct contact with my father's GP and a very formal statement from me about the problems that I saw my father facing, which I felt were not being tackled by the healthcare he was receiving. Only when I stood back and wrote down all the conditions that were present, the medicines being taken and realized that things had gone unchanged for years that should have been reviewed, did I manage to obtain the sensible care that he needed. Challenging his GP finally got the level of proactive care that was needed and has significantly improved his situation. Without this intervention, I feel things would now be very dire. Instead, a proactive relationship has developed that means my father is much more able to ask for help. He consequently feels much more "in control" and safer.

'Caring is a long-term role. Watching my parents' conditions over a period of time, it was easy to overlook a slow, gradual deterioration and assume this was the norm or to let one large illness obscure the other conditions that were developing and being ignored. It was also very easy to forget exactly "what had happened when". For instance, hospital trips, GP appointments and emergency visits tended to blend into one and be completely mistimed in history. Relying on the person you are caring for to provide this evidence didn't work because after an emergency they would generally prefer to forget it.

'For many years, my father was very resistant to receiving help from others, whether it was with household cleaning or with looking after my mother when she needed it. Attempts at getting support only occurred during emergencies, for example, when he had been taken into hospital, and usually resulted in strangers from hospital or social services being on the receiving end of suspicion. Although my father would not consider that his son is caring for him, he has seen that when I have started to take a more active involvement in organizing his care, things have improved for the better. As a result he is much more willing to accept assistance.'

Michael says that a positive effect of caring is 'becoming closer to the person you are caring for'. He has learnt several things that other carers might find useful:

- Ignoring the problems or hoping things will get better on their own doesn't work.

- Those closest to the problems, including the person caring at a distance, are not always best-placed to analyse and identify the best course of action.
- To be in a position to get help, you need to know whom to ask and trust him or her sufficiently to dare to ask for it. This is best achieved through a long-term relationship rather than a distant call-centre or disjointed approach.
- Carers need help in coming to terms with their caring role and support in planning how to deal with things *before* they develop into a crisis rather than afterwards.
- Online services, such as supermarket shopping, are invaluable for getting essentials and treats to his father, particularly when he is feeling down.

Sue

For nine years after her mother died Sue, a civil servant in London, cared for her father, who lived in Yorkshire. Initially quite independent, he became increasingly frail, yet at the time of his death, aged 91, with the support of Sue, and two professional carers, he was still living in his own home.

Sue's initial caring responsibilities mainly consisted of emotional support, providing company through regular visits, maintaining his house and shopping for him. However, after about five years, his health began to deteriorate, including several admissions to hospital. Her role then expanded to helping him to find and liaise appropriate health and social services. She also visited him most weekends and often spent several weeks in the family home when he was hospitalized or ill.

'After one hospital stay, he was allocated a social worker,' she says, 'who persuaded him that in order to stay at home, he needed additional support.' Carers provided by social services in his area were contracted-out to private companies and individuals and her father's carers came from a small local company. Initially one carer, Betty, visited once a week, then as Sue's father's needs intensified, the hours increased and the support provided expanded to two carers and included personal care. In the last year of his life, they were visiting him three times a day.

'The continuity of care was important,' Sue explains. 'He knew what times they would visit him and that it would be either Betty or Jean. As a result, he built up a good relationship with them. They were very skilled and could get him to do all sorts of things that he refused to consider when I suggested them. Although I was grateful to them, I found it galling how compliant he was with them and so resistant with me! I think that once a system of professional care has been established, it is important to keep this going even when family members are visiting. It imbeds the routine in the way of life and gives the carer a break/time to concentrate on other aspects of their relationship with the person being cared for.'

Sue's father also had a community alarm system operated by social services, which she says, 'worked very well. The two professional carers were included on the list of people to contact, which was useful given the distance, and one of them did turn out once or twice in the middle of the night to help him. Obviously there was cost involved, but I didn't care as long as help could be summoned when needed.' Sue also had some support from her aunt, who visited her father once a week. 'The neighbours were helpful too. By lunchtime, if they hadn't seen him moving about, they would go and check he was okay. They were willing to do more,' she says, 'but he would never let them in. I think he was afraid of them knowing his business or going through his things.'

Day centres and sitting services to provide company in the person's own home were available, but Sue's father wasn't interested. 'He did sometimes attend a weekly luncheon club run by the local club – despite the fact that the participants were mostly women, which he didn't like! He also had a period of respite care towards the end of his life, while I was on holiday in America. It was a lovely place that didn't have an institutional feel, but he had to be persuaded to try it. When I came back, I felt quite guilty because it was clear he hadn't had a wonderful time, even though they had looked after him well. However, when I talked to him it became apparent he had participated in activities and talked to people – so he may have not wanted to admit to me that he had enjoyed himself in case I tried to make him move there permanently.

'I would say to other carers, if you are offered help, take it. Caring can drive you potty, however much you love the person, so if someone offers to sit with the person you are caring for, even for a short time, to give you a break, take that opportunity. Also, if you can, try to take the person you are caring for out from time to time. My father used to like to go for a ride in the car and look at things even though we never stopped anywhere.'

While Sue feels she had a lot of support from social services, she thinks that carers need greater recognition and better services. 'Sometimes it isn't about a lot of money, but the way you give things out or make things accessible. Sometimes the help is there if you know where to find it, but the processes are so complex or hard to locate that you give up before you get there. It is also about other people appreciating what you do – a role that other family members or friends could play without having to do any of the "hands on" caring. It helps a lot, especially to lessen isolation, if they just phone up occasionally and ask the carer how they are.

'You have your ups and downs as a carer, but it can also be a very rewarding experience. I learnt many things as a carer – such as how the system works and what you can and can't do – which has recently made me a useful resource to my cousin who is now caring for his mother, who has advanced cancer. I can empathize with what he is going through. I also take what I learnt from caring for Dad and it helps me cope with how I feel about my aunt's situation.

'I feel I did the best I could for my father, given that he wouldn't accept a lot of things that were on offer. Sometimes I wonder if I could have done more, but living with him wouldn't have worked for either of us. However, I think that I must have done something right for him to have lived so long at home after my mother died.'

11

Young carers

Although most carers will be adults, children and teenagers can sometimes find themselves caring for a parent, grandparent or sibling – either by helping others in the family or by doing most of the work themselves, including:

- physical care – helping their relative with personal tasks such as washing, lifting, toileting, giving medication;
- emotional support;
- housework and shopping;
- finance;
- looking out for them or staying with them to ensure they don't hurt themselves;
- accompanying them to appointments – if English is not the first language in their community, this can include interpreting for their relative.

Most young carers love the person they are caring for and want to help them. The experience can have very positive outcomes for their personal development but the physical, emotional and social impact can also be enormous, particularly if the caring burden is considerable, they are the sole carer or unsupported.

The term 'young carer' is used to describe 'children and young people aged under 21 who look after someone in his or her family who has an illness, disability, mental health or substance problem'.[35] The 2001 census estimated that there are at least 175,000 young carers in the UK, including 13,000 caring for over 50 hours per week. However, many health and social care professionals and organizations working with them believe this number is much higher. For instance, the Princess Royal Trust for Carers says that the census does not include alcohol or drug problems and because of the stigma attached to these conditions, many young carers remain hidden.

If you are a young carer, it is crucial that you get the support you need. Your local authority should ensure that your education, development and well-being are not affected and that you do not have to take on similar levels of caring responsibilities to adults.[36] This chapter discusses some of the key issues affecting young carers and the services that are available to help.

Fear of coming forward

Sometimes young carers and their families are reluctant to make themselves known to services that could help because they are afraid they may be separated if they do so. In most cases, the role of health and social services will be to support the family so they can stay together. If you are a young carer and are worried about this issue, but need support, you could start by talking to a confidential telephone helpline, such as Childline, emailing the Princess Royal Trust for Carers or looking at young carer websites and discussion boards. See pages 89–91 and Useful addresses for further details.

Health and emotional well-being

The health of young carers can often be severely affected by their caring responsibilities. They may experience difficulties through:

- lack of sleep;
- tiredness;
- difficulties with concentration;
- emotional stress – including anger, guilt, blaming themselves;
- depression and anxiety.

There can be a lack of awareness among many health and social care professionals and schools about the needs of young carers, and as a result services to help them can be limited. It is to be hoped that this is changing, if the growing number of young carer initiatives are anything to go by. However, services should be available to help ease the burden. See Chapter 3: Healthcare professionals and Chapter 4: Community care.

Some young carers find they spend a lot of time on their own because their parents' attention has to be so focused on the relative being cared for. As a result, it is important to ensure they have times with their parents or other relatives specifically devoted to them.

One carer described how a doctor involved in the care of her disabled child, who had a life-limiting condition, recognized the needs of her other children and arranged for one of them, who had anxieties about her sibling's illness and death, to receive support from a cancer charity. 'She had two years of very good support and it made a big difference. He was looking at the bigger picture. He recognized there might be other strains for other members of the family as well as his patient.'

Education

According to the Princess Royal Trust for Carers, almost a third of young carers have serious educational problems, with many failing to attain any GCSEs at all. Factors that can affect them include bullying, loneliness, isolation, difficulties keeping up with their schoolwork and missing school because of their responsibilities.

Ruth thinks that now more disabled children are educated in mainstream educational establishments, schools need to be more aware of the needs of young carers. 'For example, it can be hard to get a disabled sibling ready on time and other children can be penalized for being late through no fault of their own. Concentration may also be affected by being kept awake by a sibling who doesn't sleep.'

Make sure that the school is aware of your situation and any difficulties that may arise as a result of your caring responsibilities or having a relative in the family with disabilities.

Social life

The social life of young carers can be severely limited for many reasons. They may not be able to go out with their friends because they are needed at home. The restrictions of the family finances may mean they are not able to afford holidays and other leisure activities. Isolation and loneliness are also common because many find it hard to fit in or are at odds with their peers because of their situation.

Many young carers benefit from talking to and spending time with others of the same age who are in a similar position. This may be through a young carers' project, telephone contact or Internet forums.

Young carers' projects, often run by carers or voluntary organizations, can provide opportunities to have fun at evening clubs, weekends away and holidays involving other young carers. They also have people who will listen to you and are on your side when you need to talk to someone and can provide information to help you and your family. The Children's Society: Young Carers Initiative (see p. 90) has a list on its website.

Bereavement

Bereavement issues are another area of great concern for young carers, especially when their relative has a terminal or life-limiting condition. Services to help are available from several organizations including Cruse, Help the Hospices and Winston's Wish. (See Chapter 12: Stopping caring.)

Young carers may also have feelings of sadness and loss while they are caring because their lives have changed considerably as a result, or because the person being cared for can no longer do things with them that they used to do.

Recognition of young carers

Until recently, young carers' needs often went unrecognized. Although there is still considerable work to be done in this area, the situation is improving with carers' organizations and voluntary organizations concerned with particular health conditions developing information and support services, specifically for young carers.

There is also a Young Carers Research Group at Loughborough University, which conducts high-quality research, evaluation and consultancy on all aspects relating to young carers. Their research has influenced law and policy and good practice and led to the development of young carers' projects across the UK. For more information, see <www.lboro.ac.uk/departments/ss/centres/YCRG/>.

Finding support

If you are a young carer and are finding it hard to cope, it is important that you find someone to talk to who can help you find the support you need. This might be a parent, other relative, family friend, teacher at your school, health or social care professional with whom you feel comfortable, a carers'/voluntary organization or a young carers' worker. Your local carers' organization or social services should be able to advise you further, or contact one of the following organizations which focus on young carers' issues. They would also help parents or relatives concerned about a young carer.

The Princess Royal Trust for Carers actively campaigns for better services for young carers. Their whole-family approach aims to address the underlying reasons why some young people take on caring responsibilities inappropriate for their age.

The Trust's young carers' services provide advice, mentoring, support with education, clubs and holidays to young carers. Its website for young carers <www.youngcarers.net> contains lots of information for young carers plus discussion boards, regular chat sessions, agony aunt forums and archives plus a free monthly young carers' newsletter. Young carers (18 and under) can email questions about caring to youngcarers@carers.org and a young online carers' worker will respond, usually within a day.

Many of the Trust's local carers' centres have young carers' projects or have been involved with other organizations within their local area in setting one up.

Barnardo's is a voluntary organization for children, which runs several projects in the UK that support young carers and keep families together. On their website are video clips and stories of young carers involved in some of their projects.

Childline is a free 24-hour helpline for children and young people in the UK, staffed by counsellors, who will listen to any problem that they have at any time and help them find solutions.

The Children's Society is a voluntary organization that campaigns on issues affecting children and provides projects to help those who need extra help. The Children's Society: Young Carers Initiative is a website for young carers <www.youngcarer.com>, which provides information on young carers' issues and projects nationwide.

Many of the Crossroads – Caring for Carers schemes support young carers by providing them with support and enabling them to have a break from caring by facilitating participation in leisure and cultural activities.

NCH, the children's charity supports young carers through projects to help children caring for a sick or disabled relative to cope with the additional pressures they face. It also campaigns for better services for young carers and raises awareness about their needs.

Young Minds promotes the mental health of children. They have a national telephone helpline, Young Minds Parents Information Service, which provides information and advice for any adult concerned about the mental health of a child or young person. Their publications include a book for young children, *The Wise Mouse*, which explains what it is like to have a parent or family member who has a mental illness. A new project, Minority Voices, will look into access to mental health services for young people from black and minority ethnic communities.

Many voluntary organizations for specific health conditions have recognized the needs of young carers and have produced information or services. For instance, the MS Society worked with the Princess Royal

Trust for Carers on their young carers' website and has a young carers' fund for those from families on a low income to help them achieve a personal goal.

Personal experiences

Joan

Joan is the younger daughter of Anne, whose experiences of caring for her disabled daughter Anna feature in other chapters of this book. Now aged 18, she helped her parents with Anna's basic and general care. She says, 'I would do the daily things like washing, dressing, changing nappies and putting her to bed. I learnt to do her basic physiotherapy and how to give her oxygen when she was really ill. I would often help her at the weekends and when I did it I always liked to make sure that Anna was dressed nicely and that she was wearing nice clothes. I enjoyed knowing that what we were doing was making her have a nice life and got a lot out of seeing her very happy.'

Joan says it was always her choice to care for Anna and she didn't do anything she didn't want to do or felt uncomfortable doing, 'which wasn't much'. She says she admired her parents because they were able to juggle the time between Anna, Joan and their brother Robert, although there were times when she thinks perhaps she would have liked their undivided attention. Having the choice whether or not to care is a crucial issue in how well a young carer may cope with caring.

Joan thinks caring was a natural instinct for her and has decided, after her gap year in Australia, to pursue nursing as a career. She also thinks caring made her a much more open-minded person, 'because I always had to keep an open mind about everything and be very willing to adapt my own lifestyle to the changes in Anna's. I have no trouble with new circumstances because things were changing all the time and you just got used to having to deal with the new situation.'

Her friends accepted Anna without any problems. 'Two friends in particular would do things like bringing her yoghurts that she liked or a wrapper – because she liked to sit with some form of crinkly paper in her hand.' However, she says, 'new friends or those less close sometimes found it awkward. There was also one occasion when I heard that a girl's mother had said, "You need to be nice to Joan because she doesn't get enough attention at home. So she's going to struggle at school." It made me livid, because I was so angry that people could think that when they had no basis for saying it – they didn't know my family, they didn't know the background.'

Joan's secondary school was very supportive of her needs, such as time off, she says, particularly towards the end of Anna's life. She was quite close to a couple of teachers, and counselling was available, if wanted, through the school nurse. She didn't feel the need to take this up, because she was referred to a specialist children's counsellor separately.

The services that Joan found the most helpful were those provided by the local children's hospice, Rachel House, where Anna went for respite care and the family sometimes went for family weekends. 'It was nice because they had sit-down meals, Anna would have a specific carer allocated each day, the families got to socialize, and the parents got respite. There was a lovely big garden, an art room, a kitchen to bake in, a Jacuzzi, a place to retreat upstairs, entertainment and games. Also people to chat to if you wanted to. I think that a lot of the time, with these situations, you just want time out and opportunities to talk if you want to.'

Although Joan met siblings like her, who helped their parents on a voluntary basis, at the hospice, she didn't know young carers who cared for adults. She thinks there is a huge difference in your ability to cope between having the choice to care and having to. 'Being part of something like the hospice scheme where there is no pressure would be the best kind of service for young carers who have to care. A service that was just there so that if they felt they needed to use it, they could go along rather than there being a set time and date, because I think a lot of the time – if that was the case – it can feel like another chore to do. Set respite care they could look forward to would also be important.'

Joan's advice to young carers is 'to do only the things you feel happy with. Don't do something you're not happy with or that you feel is too much. Always remember that you need to think about yourself in these situations at some stage and don't be afraid to ask for help. Remember your best is always good enough.'

Crossroads – Caring for Carers

The Crossroads – Caring for Carers scheme in Brentwood Essex (mentioned earlier, pp. 67–8), provides services for young carers, including a club which provides meetings and outings, as well as a range of activities including instruction from qualified visitors such as the Fire Brigade, counselling and careers advice, and craft/drama sessions. Crossroads workers provide respite care services while they attend. May Darke, who runs the scheme, says:

'I have come across children as young as six giving care to relatives.

When a marriage breaks down, the child often takes on the caring responsibilities. They miss out on teenage experiences because they are unable to go out. They also have worries such as whether their parent is ill because of them. Many keep their situation secret because they are afraid they will be taken away. We help them to feel less alone and listen to them, as well as providing respite care.

'I think young carers should be encouraged to talk to people and let others know they are a young carer. One of my colleagues is about to start raising awareness in schools and colleges because a lot of them are not aware that children are young carers and they just think the children are just missing school for other reasons. They don't realize the child may have been up at 6.00 a.m. in the morning, got their parent ready, got their own breakfast before they went to school. So I think raising the awareness of young carers is most important and will make it easier for them to tell others that they are a young carer.'

12

Stopping caring

There may come a point at which you have to stop being a carer. Most often, this happens if the person you are caring for dies or goes to live in a residential care establishment.

Many people assume that a carer's psychological and physical health will improve when the caring role stops. While for some this may be true, many carers find stopping caring can have a huge emotional and psychological impact, particularly if their life has been wrapped around their caring role for a long time.

Residential care

Making the decision it is time to look for residential care is a difficult and complicated undertaking. Although in many cases it can be the best solution for all concerned, the emotional and practical effects on carers and other members of the family can be enormous. To ensure you find the most appropriate solution for your circumstances, it is important to find expert advice and information to help you in your search.

Residential care generally falls into three main types:

- sheltered or supported housing for people who may be able to live independently but need some support;
- residential homes for people who need help with personal care;
- nursing homes for people who need personal and nursing care.

The local social services department should advise you. (See Chapter 4: Community care.)

Voluntary organizations and welfare/benevolent organizations should provide information and some may run care homes. These include organizations focused on specific health conditions, disabled children, older people, ex-servicemen and women, particular occupations, or related to religions, ethnic backgrounds and cultures. (See Chapter 2: Sources of information and advice and Chapter 5: Finances.)

Voluntary or not-for-profit organizations that specialize in providing sheltered housing, residential or nursing home care include:

- Abbeyfield – housing with support for older people;
- Anchor Trust – housing, care and support for older people in England;
- Golden Lane Housing (affiliated to Mencap) – provision of a variety of housing solutions for people with learning disabilities;
- John Grooms – care and support services including housing, residential, nursing and respite care for disabled people and their families;
- Leonard Cheshire – residential services for many different client groups including people with acquired brain injuries, learning and cognitive impairments, progressive neurological conditions and mobility impairments;
- Sue Ryder – neurological and palliative care.

The Commission for Social Care Inspection provides information on nursing and residential homes, including inspection reports. If you are looking for homes in the other UK countries, contact the Commission's counterparts listed in Chapter 4: Community care.

The Relatives and Residents Association is a voluntary organization that exists for older people needing or living in residential care and the families and friends 'left behind'. Their services include:

- support and information via their helpline on issues to do with care homes, paying for care or complaining about the quality of care that is being provided. They also recognize that relatives often need a listening ear to cope with feelings of guilt about their perceived inability to carry on caring;
- publications including several that deal with the emotional and spiritual impact of having someone you care for go to live in residential care;
- project work on specific issues;
- influencing policy and practice;
- working with local relatives and residents groups in care homes.

Counsel and Care publish the *Complete Care Home Guide* for older people and carers who are looking for a care home or researching the options for paying for care.

Choosing a Care Home by Mary V. Goudge, an experienced matron/ manager, provides impartial practical advice on planning an elderly person's move into a care home and how to ensure that it works well for everyone concerned. Paying for care is discussed in Chapter 4: Community care.

Bereavement

If the person you have been caring for has died, there are two aspects that you will have to deal with:

- practical and financial matters;
- the emotional and physical impact on you and other members of your family.

Practical aspects

There are several legal and financial matters that must be attended to after a death. These include registering the death, arranging the funeral, sorting out the will (if there is one) and notifying various organizations and people. You may also need to sort out your own financial situation, which may change following the person's death, for instance, if you depended on financial benefits paid to the person who has died. Your local social services department, carers' organization or Citizens Advice should be able to advise you further.

The government website <www.direct.gov.uk> has sections on 'What to do after a death' and 'Financial help and support if you are bereaved (money, tax and benefits)'. This includes information on a one-off Bereavement Payment that is available to some people whose husband, wife or civil partner has died where they meet other criteria, and a one-off Funeral Payment that some families on a low income may be entitled to.

The Princess Royal Trust for Carers produces a short guide to dealing with practical issues following a death.

Dealing with the emotional aspects

Bereavement is a process that usually takes at least one to two years. Dealing with loss is always difficult and because it is a very individual experience, you have to find your own way of coping with it. Don't be hard on yourself if you find it a struggle, you feel that your life now lacks purpose or it takes you a long time to adapt to your new circumstances. Take one day at a time, allow yourself space to express your feelings – this is better than bottling them up and allowing them to fester inside you.

Bereavement can also affect your physical health. If you are not sleeping, feel very depressed, tired or overwhelmed by your feelings, it is important that you consult your GP. As well as prescribing treatments to help you cope with these, he or she can refer you to other healthcare professionals and services.

Many former carers say that talking to a counsellor or people in a similar position has helped them enormously with their feelings and the transition to a life after caring.

The Royal College of Psychiatrists produce several publications on bereavement that mainly focus on the emotional and psychological aspects of bereavement.

Cruse Bereavement Care is a charity that supports bereaved people through counselling, support, information, advice, education and training services. It has a specific website for young bereaved people <www.rd4u.org.uk>.

The Compassionate Friends is an organization of bereaved parents and their families who offer understanding, support and encouragement to others after the death of a child or children through a helpline, local groups, publications, one-to-one visiting, telephone and letter contact, and bereaved siblings' website.

In addition to providing support to people with terminal illnesses and life-limiting conditions in their lifetime, hospices also provide support to their families including bereavement care. Contact Help the Hospices or the Association of Children's Hospices for more information.

The National Association of Bereavement Services can provide you with details of most appropriate bereavement services available to you in your local area.

Winston's Wish supports bereaved children and young people up to the age of 18. Its activities include a helpline and specialized residential weekend groups.

Building a new future

Building a new future takes time. Your local carers' organizations should be able to help you consider options and plan for the future. They may also have specific services or support groups for former carers. Voluntary organizations for the specific health condition you have been coping with should also be able to help.

If you are on benefits such as Carers' Allowance and Carers' Premium, these can continue for eight weeks after the person you are caring for has died. You will then be expected to register for work unless you are ill or past working age. You should do this to protect your national insurance record and to check whether you qualify for Jobseeker's Allowance, paid to men under 65 and women under 60 who meet the criteria and who are actively seeking work.[37]

Support and incentives may be available to help you get back to work. Contact your local Jobcentre Plus for information <www.jobcentreplus.gov.uk>. Citizens Advice can also advise on your rights and financial matters.

Personal experiences

Anne and Joan

Anne cared for her daughter, Anna, until her death at the age of 17 in 2001.

'I wasn't able to take very much time off after Anna died. I had one week's bereavement leave and not much understanding from my employers, then I was forced back to work. This was because all the benefits stopped, so there was a big *tranche* of income that just went bang. I became increasingly disillusioned with my job teaching English as a foreign language to adults. Also I think being in the environment where I had been throughout Anna's life reminded me of it on a daily basis. I eventually became very depressed.'

It was at this point that Anne's career took a turn in a completely different, ultimately very rewarding direction that involved using her professional and caring experiences. 'My husband saw an advert for a job as a paediatric project officer for Contact a Family. He said, "You're not going to believe this job – it could have been written for you." Nowhere would you have found a job that sat so perfectly with my caring and teaching experiences. When I first started, I said to my boss, "I can't wait to get into work every day, I feel so excited." I still feel like that about it.'

Anne's post, funded by the Big Lottery, is running a project called 'Parents and Paediatricians Together', which is a partnership between Contact a Family and the Royal College of Paediatrics and Child Health. There are two aims – information and participation.

Information involves facilitating the flow of information from health professionals to families. 'What we are asking professionals to do is to signpost families to us as a huge resource in terms of information and support. So professionals don't have to reinvent the wheel, they have the confidence to know that whatever the families' information needs – benefits, welfare rights, housing, education – we can provide this or know someone who can. If we don't, we'll find it.'

Participation is about parental involvement, i.e. having their voices heard and views used to shape the delivery of child health services. Anne says, 'It can be very empowering giving people the resources and the opportunities to use their experiences and participate in initiatives at every step of the way.'

Joan, Anne's younger daughter, says she felt at a loose end after Anna died – not just because of the loss of her sister. 'I was lost without the caring role,' she says. 'I felt that something I enjoyed doing was missing as well as Anna, which was unsettling. I missed helping getting her up and there were tiny things about her care routine that I'd remember. Within a year of her death, I decided that I wanted to be a nurse because I liked these caring things so much. My advice to young carers who are at this point would be to start doing the things you have always wanted to do with your own life. You could also consider finding an occupation such as physiotherapy or nursing that allows you to use what you liked about caring in a positive way.'

For a long time after Anna died, Joan didn't want to talk about her caring experiences. However, now that she has left school and is moving on to her adult life, she has started to think about and share them with other people.

A common feeling among carers, that Anne and Joan both felt, is not wanting the person they cared for to be forgotten and for their caring experiences to be used in a positive way to help others – perhaps by contributing stories to books like this or working with a voluntary organization as a volunteer or staff member. Writing about your experiences or creating a memory book can help. Joan found a particularly personal way: 'I wanted something that would signify the fact that I was moving on,' Joan says. 'I had a tattoo put on my foot for my eighteenth birthday. It is a dragonfly from a story, *Waterbugs and Dragonflies*,[38] which Rachel House, the hospice where Anna had respite care and we spent time as a family, uses to explain the concept of death to children – so I have Anna marked on me now forever.'

Audrey

Audrey Jenkinson is an actress who had to put her career on hold to care for her mother who had a stroke and her father who had been diagnosed with cancer. When they died, she felt a considerable 'void' in her life and wondered how other people coped in similar situations. She travelled throughout the UK, interviewing former carers to ask them how they rebuilt their lives. The result was a book, *Past Caring: The beginning not the end*, which contains many former carers' stories and a 12-step recovery guide.

Conclusion

I hope that the contents of this book will help you to find the information and support you need to help you as a carer. As the stories and experiences of the carers demonstrate, caring isn't easy, but it is possible to cope, provided you have the right support and information to meet your particular needs.

If you are going to cope with the challenges that caring throws at you, you must look after your own health and well-being. I know that it can be very difficult to find the time or space to do this, but if you don't, your health and emotional welfare may be compromised to such an extent that you are no longer able to care.

The following tips have been compiled from discussions with carers while researching this book and when I worked at the Parkinson's Disease Society.[39]

Make sure you have the information and services you need

Hopefully the health/social care professionals involved in your care will provide you with the information and contact numbers you require. If this does not happen, contact the organizations highlighted in this book that seem appropriate for your needs. Even if you don't want information or help at the moment, knowing where to go when you need to is important.

Ask for a community care assessment for the person you are caring for and a carer's assessment

This will ensure that the needs of the person you are caring for, and your own needs as a carer, are recognized, and services provided to help you. Unfortunately, what is available is very dependent on your local area. One carer stressed the importance of continuing to ask for something, even if it wasn't available, because if enough people ask, this may lead to provision. Another said that it was essential to know your rights and what health/social care services should be providing as this put you in a better position to ask for what you need and argue if you don't receive it.

Keep banging on the door

This was a cry that was echoed by every carer that I spoke to. *Anne* says, 'Things will not land on your plate, you only get things if you ask. Unfortunately sometimes those that shout loudest get. Use logical arguments rather than just getting angry. Where possible, it pays to work with the professionals, rather than against them.'

Arm yourself with self-management strategies

Gather as much information about the condition and caring as you can. Courses to help you with self-management strategies include the Expert Patient Programme Community Interest Company or carers'/voluntary organizations. (See Chapter 6: Employment and education for carers.)

Keep a diary or record

Keep a diary or some record of the symptoms and difficulties that the person you are caring for has, and the details of your caring role. This can help you keep track of how living with disability or illness affects you and help you when dealing with health and social care professionals.

Check what financial benefits you may be entitled to

Don't assume that health/social care professionals will automatically tell you if you are entitled to benefits. Several carers I spoke to while writing this book knew of people who had gone for years without benefits they were entitled to, such as Disability Living Allowance, because no one had told them they were entitled to claim it. (See Chapter 5: Finances.)

Accept your feelings and talk about what you are doing

Most carers say that talking about their feelings and what they are doing makes caring much easier. Some people prefer to talk to the person they are caring for or family and friends. However, some people also find it helps to talk to someone outside the family. See Chapter 7: Emotional, psychological and spiritual impact.

Anne says, 'Network madly by talking to people. Don't make yourself more isolated by withdrawing into your shell.'

Make it clear what you would like to do

Don't assume because you are a carer that you have to do everything single-handedly. Make it clear what you are and aren't willing to do. This will prevent unrealistic expectations and resentment building up. Although it may seem impossible from where you sit, alternatives often can be found for the tasks that you aren't able or don't want to do.

Where possible, encourage independence on the part of the person you are caring for, even if this means activities take longer. This will improve their self-esteem and lessen your caring burden.

Have contact with other carers

This will provide you with information, ideas, knowledge and support from people in a similar position. *Eva* says, 'Sometimes you don't talk about your caring role at all, you talk about ordinary life but you don't constantly have to explain because you are with people who understand.'

Maintain your own health and keep time for yourself

A common danger is for the carer to concentrate all their energies on caring for the person and to neglect their own health. However hard it is to do so, make sure that you accept help from other people and have regular breaks from caring. Eating well, exercising regularly and learning relaxation techniques are all vital parts of this process. If you find your caring responsibilities overwhelming or you feel depressed and exhausted, talk to your GP as a matter of urgency.

Don't make caring and the health condition in question the sole focus of your life

Make sure that you and the person you are caring for have things that you like to do together that are not about the health condition. Even if these pursuits need to be adapted, try to keep on doing them. Having times away from each other to pursue individual interests is also important.

Try to keep your sense of humour

Almost without exception, everyone I talked to said that keeping their sense of humour and seeing the funny side of things helped them cope with caring.

Messages for health/social care professionals and policy-makers

Recognition of the important role carers play in supporting their relatives and friends is increasing but much more work is needed. Many carers struggle with very difficult situations and receive very little support. The following key factors, highlighted by carers I have talked to, if addressed would greatly improve quality of life for all carers.

Access to information for carers should be easier

Health and social care professionals can play a major role in facilitating this and can be extremely effective when it works well. Yet the experience of carers I talked to suggests that many don't know what is available and aren't good at signposting. One carer said, 'It isn't about them knowing everything but just where I can find it.' Many also talked about the frustrations of misinformation and being passed from pillar to post and still not getting to the person they need. An articulate or assertive carer will persist in looking for the information but many are not in this position. If they receive a negative or unhelpful response when they do try, they will be put off and never try again. Even the proactive ones may find it hard to ask for help about an issue that has a lot of meaning for them.

Your attitude and approach to the families you work with can make or break your relationship with them

Ruth says, 'The professionals that have been most helpful to me, have been the ones that haven't said, "Poor you". Instead, if they say they will do something for me, they have done it, got back to me about why they haven't done it or passed it to the right person to deal with. They have treated Alice and me with respect and made enough difference to enable me to keep going quite positively in some respects.'

Having a key worker can make a tremendous difference to quality of life of carers and the person they are caring for

This can also enable regular contact with the family to ensure they have the support they need. *Ruth* says, 'I would have liked more contact regularly. Someone to just see how I was. I feel I am always asking for something. It would be much better for someone to say the service is here and if you don't want it, that's fine, but it's here and you are entitled to it. The feeling I am always given is that I am privileged if I get anything.'

Make sure the information you provide is available in different formats

This includes community languages appropriate to your area and service. Remember that written information may not be the most appropriate for some communities.

Adequate respite care services are essential

These ensure the well-being of carers and prevent depression and/or burnout. One carer said, 'They seem so varied and there doesn't seem to be any kind of pattern to them. Some people do well, others don't.'

The benefits system could be simpler and fairer

One carer asked why carers of children have to fill in Disability Living Allowance forms on such a regular basis. Another said they felt there should be a sliding scale for benefits such as carers' allowance according to the nature of the caring role undertaken. The system also needs to recognize and provide for the additional burden carried by a considerable proportion of carers who care for more than one person.

The vital role that professional carers play in supporting informal carers and the people they care for should have great value in society

One carer said professional carers were devalued by society and poorly paid, yet 'they are the people that informal carers need to have confidence in so that they can let go when they need to'.

Informal carers save the government billions of pounds through the support they provide

There must be greater recognition of their role, easier access to support and information services and much more money deployed to provide additional resources to help them. It was suggested that a 'tsar' to champion carers' rights within the health service should be appointed alongside those that already exist for health specialities such as cancer, mental health and older people.

Useful addresses

Carers' organizations

Carers UK
20–25 Glasshouse Yard
London EC1A 4JS
CarersLine: 0808 808 7777
(Wednesday/Thursday 10 a.m. to 12
noon and 2 to 4 p.m.)
Tel.: 020 7490 8818
Website: www.carersuk.org

Crossroads – Caring for Carers
10 Regent Place
Rugby
Warwickshire CV21 2PN
Tel.: 0845 450 0350
Website: www.crossroads.org.uk

The Princess Royal Trust for Carers
142 Minories
London EC3N 1LB
Tel.: 020 7480 7788
Website: www.carers.org

Voluntary organizations for specific conditions

AbilityNet
PO Box 94
Warwick
Helpline (Freephone: 0800 269545
Website: www.abilitynet.org.uk

Action on Elder Abuse
Astral House
1268 London Road
Norbury
London SW16 4ER
Tel: 020 8765 7000
Helpline: 0808 808 8141
Website: www.elderabuse.org.uk

Age Concern Cymru (Wales)
Ty John Pathy
13–14 Neptune Court
Vanguard Way
Cardiff CF24 5PJ
Tel.: 029 2043 1555
Website: www.accymru.org.uk

Age Concern England
Astral House
1268 London Road
London SW16 4ER
Information Line: 0800 00 99 66
(7 a.m. to 7 p.m. every day)
Website: www.ageconcern.org.uk

Age Concern Northern Ireland
3 Lower Crescent
Belfast BT7 1NR
Tel.: 028 9024 5729
Website: www.ageconcernni.org

Age Concern Scotland
Causewayside House
160 Causewayside
Edinburgh EH9 1PR
Tel.: 0845 833 0200
Helpline for Older People: 0845 125
9732 (10 a.m. to 4 p.m., Monday to
Friday)
Website: www.ageconcernscotland.
org.uk

Alzheimer Scotland – Action on Dementia
22 Drumsheugh Gardens
Edinburgh EH3 7RN
Tel.: 0131 243 1453
Helpline (24-hour): 0808 808 3000
Website: www.alzscot.org

Alzheimer's Society
Gordon House
10 Greencoat Place
London SW1P 1PH.
Tel.: 020 7306 0606
Helpline 0845 300 0336 (8.30 a.m. to
6.30 p.m., Monday to Friday)
Website: www.alzheimers.org.uk

Arthritis Care
18 Stephenson Way
London NW1 2HD
Tel.: 020 7380 6500
Helpline: 0808 800 4050
Information Line (24-hour): 0845 600
6868
Website: www.arthritiscare.org.uk
Hotels: www.arthritiscarehotels.org.uk

**The Association for Spina Bifida
and Hydrocephalus (ASBAH)**
42 Park Road
Peterborough PE1 2UQ
Tel: 01733 555988
Helpline: 0845 450 7755 (Monday to
Friday)
Website: www.asbah.org

Barnardo's
Tanners Lane
Barkingside
Ilford
Essex IG6 1QG
Tel.: 020 8550 8822
Website: www.barnardos.org.uk
(Shared with regional offices below)

Barnardo's Northern Ireland
542–544 Upper Newtownards Road
Belfast BT4 3HE
Tel.: 028 9067 2366

Barnardo's Scotland
235 Corstorphine Road
Edinburgh
EH12 7AR
Tel.: 0131 334 9893

Barnardo's Wales
Trident Court
East Moors Road
Cardiff
CF24 5TD
Tel.: 029 2049 3387

The Brain and Spine Foundation
7 Winchester House
Kennington Park
Cranmer Road
London SW9 6EJ
Tel.: 020 7582 8712
Website: www.brainandspine.
org.uk

British Heart Foundation
14 Fitzhardinge Street
London W1H 6DH
Tel.: 020 7935 0185
Heart Information Line: 08450 70
80 70 (9 a.m. to 5 p.m., Monday to
Friday)
Website: www.bhf.org.uk

Cancerbackup
3 Bath Place
Rivington Street
London EC2A 3JR
Helpline: 0808 800 1234
Website: www.cancerbackup.org.uk

CLIC Sargent
Tel: 0845 301 0031 (general enquiries)
Child Cancer Helpline: 0800 197 0068
(9 a.m. to 5 p.m., Monday to Friday)
Website: www.clicsargent.org.uk

Provides support and care for children
and young people with cancer, and
their families. Regional offices detailed
below, but all share the same website.

CLIC Sargent (Bristol office)
Abbey Wood Business Park
Filton
Bristol BS34 7JU
Tel.: 0117 311 2600

CLIC Sargent (London office)
Griffin House
161 Hammersmith Road
London W6 8SG
Tel.: 020 8752 2800

CLIC Sargent (Northern Ireland)
3rd Floor, 31 Bruce Street
Belfast BT2 7JD
Tel.: 028 9072 5780

CLIC Sargent (Scotland)
5th Floor, Mercantile Chambers
53 Bothwell Street
Glasgow G2 6TS
Tel.: 0141 572 5700

Counsel and Care
Twyman House
16 Bonny Street
London NW1 9PG
Tel.: 020 7241 8555
Advice line: 0845 300 7585 (10 a.m.
to 12 noon/2 p.m. to 4 p.m., Monday
to Friday)
Website: www.counselandcare.org.uk

Provides support for older people and
their families and carers.

Depression Alliance (England)
212 Spitfire Studios
63–71 Collier Street
London N1 9BE
Tel.: 0845 123 23 20 (publications
line for both England and Scotland)
Website: www.depressionalliance.org

Depression Alliance (Scotland)
3 Grosvenor Gardens
Edinburgh EH12 5JU
Tel.: 0131 467 3050
Website: www.dascot.org

Diabetes UK
Macleod House
10 Parkway
London NW1 7AA
Tel.: 020 7424 1000
Website: www.diabetes.org.uk

Down's Syndrome Association
Langdon Down Centre
2a Langdon Park
Teddington TW11 9PS
Tel.: 0845 230 0372
Website:www.downs-syndrome.org.uk

The Dystonia Society
Camelford House
89 Albert Embankment
London SE1 7TP
Tel.: 0845 458 6211 (general
information)
Helpline: 0845 458 6322
Website: www.dystonia.org.uk

Enable Scotland
6th Floor, 7 Buchanan Street
Glasgow G1 3HL
Tel.: 0141 226 4541
Website www.enable.org.uk

Provides support across Scotland for
children and adults with learning
difficulties.

Eurordis
Plateforme Maladies Rares
102, rue Didot
75014 Paris
France
Tel.: +33 (1) 56.53.52.10
Website: www.eurordis.org

**Foundation for People with
Learning Difficulties**
(see the **Mental Health Foundation**)

Help the Aged (England)
207–221 Pentonville Road
London N1 9UZ
Tel.: 020 7278 1114
SeniorLine: 0808 800 6565
Website: www.helptheaged.org.uk
(Website shared by regional offices
detailed below)

Help the Aged (Northern Ireland)
Ascot House
Shaftesbury Square
Belfast BT2 7DB
Tel.: 028 9023 0666

Help the Aged (Scotland)
11 Granton Square
Edinburgh EH5 1HX
Tel.: 0131 551 6331

Help the Aged (Wales)
12 Cathedral Road
Cardiff CF11 9LJ
Tel.: 029 2034 6550

Huntington's Disease Association
Down Stream Building
1 London Bridge
London SE1 9BG
Tel.: 020 7022 1950
Website: www.hda.org.uk

Macmillan Cancer Support
89 Albert Embankment
London SE1 7UQ
CancerLine: 0808 808 2020 (free, 9
a.m. to 10 p.m.)
YouthLine: 0808 808 0800 (free, 9
a.m. to 10 p.m.)
Website: www.macmillan.org.uk

MDF The BiPolar Organisation
Castle Works
21 St George's Road
London SE1 6ES
Tel.: 08456 340 540
Website: www.mdf.org.uk

Mencap Cymru
31 Lambourne Crescent
Cardiff Business Park
Llanishen
Cardiff CF14 5GF
Tel.: 029 2074 7588
Wales Learning Disability Helpline:
0808 8000 300

Mencap (England)
123 Golden Lane
London EC1Y 0RT
Tel.: 020 7454 0454
Learning disability helpline: 0808 808
1111
Website: www.mencap.org.uk (Shared
by regional offices detailed below)

Mencap Northern Ireland
Segal House
4 Annadale Avenue
Belfast BT7 3JH
Tel.: 028 9069 1351

**The Mental Health Foundation
(London office)**
9th Floor, Sea Containers House
20 Upper Ground
London SE1 9QB
Tel.: 020 7803 1101
Website: www.mhf.org.uk (Website
shared with Scottish office below)

**The Mental Health Foundation
(Scotland)**
Merchants House
30 George Square
Glasgow G2 1EG
Tel.: 0141 572 0125

Mind
15–19 Broadway
London E15 4BQ
Tel.: 020 8519 2122
MindinfoLine: 08457 660163
Website: www.mind.org.uk

Motor Neurone Disease Association
PO Box 246
Northampton NN1 2PR
Tel.: 01604 250505
Helpline: 08457 626262
Website: www.mndassociation.org

Multiple Sclerosis (MS) Society
MS National Centre
372 Edgware Road
London NW2 6ND
Tel.: 020 8438 0700
Website: www.mssociety.org.uk

Muscular Dystrophy Campaign
National Office
7–11 Prescott Place
London SW4 6BS
Tel.: 020 7720 8055
Website: www.muscular-dystrophy.
org

The National Autistic Society
393 City Road
London EC1V 1NG
Tel.: 020 7833 2299
Autism Helpline: 0845 070 4004
Website: www.nas.org.uk (Shared
with regional offices detailed below)

**The National Autistic Society
(Northern Ireland)**
57a Botanic Avenue
Belfast BT7 1JL
Tel.: 028 9023 6235

**The National Autistic Society
(Scotland)**
Central Chambers
First Floor, 109 Hope Street
Glasgow G2 6LL
Tel.: 0141 221 8090

**The National Autistic Society
(Wales)**
6–7 Village Way
Greenmeadow Springs
Business Park
Tongwynlais
Cardiff CF15 7NE
Tel.: 029 2062 9312

NCH, the children's charity
85 Highbury Park
London N5 1UD
Tel.: 020 7704 7000
Website: www.nch.org.uk (Website
shared with regional offices below)

NCH Cymru (Wales)
St David's Court
68a Cowbridge Road East
Cardiff CF11 9DN
Tel.: 029 2022 2127

NCH Northern Ireland
10 Heron Road
Belfast BT3 9LE
Tel.: 028 9046 0500

NCH Scotland
City Park
368 Alexandra Parade
Glasgow G31 3AU.
Tel.: 0141 550 9010

Parkinson's Disease Society
215 Vauxhall Bridge Road
London SW1V 1EJ
Tel.: 020 7931 8080
Advisory Line: 0808 800 0303
(Monday to Friday, 9.30 a.m. to 9
p.m.; Saturday 9.30 a.m. to 5.30 p.m.)
Website: www.parkinsons.org.uk

Rethink
28 Castle Street
Kingston-Upon-Thames
Surrey KT1 1SS
Tel.: 0845 456 0455 (general)
020 8974 6814 (National Advice
Service, 10 a.m. to 3 p.m., Monday
to Friday)
Website: www.rethink.org

SANE
First Floor, Cityside House
40 Adler Street
London E1 1EE
Tel.: 0845 767 8000 (SANELINE, 1
p.m. to 11 p.m. every day)
Website: www.sane.org.uk

Scope
6 Market Road
London N7 9PW
Tel.: 0808 800 3333
Website: www.scope.org.uk

The Stroke Association
240 City Road
London EC1V 2PR
Helpline: 0845 3033 100
Website: www.stroke.org.uk

Young Minds
48–50 St John Street
London EC1M 4DG
Tel.: 020 7336 8445
Website: www.youngminds.org.uk

Other useful organizations

The Abbeyfield Society
Abbeyfield House
53 Victoria Street
St Albans
Herts AL1 3UW
Tel.: 01727 857536
Website: www.abbeyfield.com

Helps with the provision of low-cost
retirement housing.

The Anchor Trust (homes and care)
Chancery House
St Nicholas Way
Sutton
Surrey SM1 1JB
Tel.: 020 8652 1900
Website: www.anchor.org.uk

Association of Charity Officers
Five Ways
57–59 Hatfield Road
Potters Bar
Herts EN6 1HS
Tel.: 01707 651777
Website: www.aco.uk.net

National umbrella body for charities
that provide aid and advice to
individuals in need. Their special-
interest group, the Occupational
Benevolent Funds Alliance, can be
contacted via www.joblinks.org.uk.

**The Association of Children's
Hospices**
First Floor, Canningford House
36 Victoria Street
Bristol BS1 6BY
Tel.: 0117 989 7820
Website: www.childhospice.org.uk

Break
Davison House
1 Montague Road
Sheringham
Norfolk NR26 8WN
Tel.: 01263 822161
Website: www.break-charity.org

The British Association/College of Occupational Therapists
106–114 Borough High Street
Southwark
London SE1 1LB
Tel.: 020 7357 6480
Website: www.cot.org.uk

The British Association for Counselling and Psychotherapy (BACP)
BACP House
15 St John's Business Park
Lutterworth
Leics LE17 4HB
Tel.: 0870 443 5252
Website: www.bacp.co.uk

British Association of Social Workers
16 Kent Street
Birmingham B5 6RD
Tel.: 0121 622 3911
Website: www.basw.co.uk

British Complementary Medicine Association (BCMA)
PO Box 5122
Bournemouth BH8 0WG
Tel.: 0845 345 5977
Website: www.bcma.co.uk

British Dietetic Association
5th Floor, Charles House
148/9 Great Charles Street
Queensway
Birmingham B3 3HT
Tel.: 0121 200 8080
Website: www.bda.uk.com

The British Psychological Society
St Andrew's House
48 Princess Road East
Leicester LE1 7DR
Tel.: 0116 254 9568
Website: www.bps.org.uk

CareAware
PO Box 8
Manchester M30 9NY
Tel.: 08705 134925
Website: www.careaware.co.uk

Care and Repair Cymru
Norbury House
Norbury Road
Fairwater
Cardiff CF5 3AS
Tel.: 029 20576 286
Website: www.careandrepair.org.uk

Care and Repair (England)
The Renewal Trust Business Centre
3 Hawksworth Street
Nottingham NG3 2EG
Tel.: 0115 950 6500
Website: www.careandrepair-england.org.uk

Care and Repair Forum Scotland
135 Buchanan Street
Suite 2.5
Glasgow G1 2JA
Tel.: 0141 221 9879
Website: www.careandrepairscotland.co.uk

Care Standards Inspectorate for Wales
4/5 Charnwood Court
Heol Billingsley
Parc Nantgarw
Nantgarw CF15 7QZ
Tel.: 01443 848450
Website: www.csiw.wales.gov.uk

Centre for Accessible Environments
70 South Lambeth Road
London SW8 1RL
Tel.: 020 7840 0125
Website: www.cae.org.uk

Charity Search
25 Portview Road
Avonmouth
Bristol BS11 9LD
Tel.: 0117 982 4060 (Monday to Friday, 10 a.m. to 4 p.m.)

Chartered Society of Physiotherapists
14 Bedford Row
London WC1R 4ED
Tel.: 020 7306 6666
Website: www.csp.org.uk

ChildLine
Tel.: 0800 1111
Website: www.childline.org.uk

The Children's Society
Edward Rudolf House
Margery Street
London WC1X 0JL
Tel.: 0845 300 1128
Website: www.childrenssociety.org.uk

Citizens Advice (Operating name of the National Association of Citizens Advice Bureaux)
115–123 Pentonville Road
London N1 9LZ
Tel.: 020 7833 2181
Website: www.adviceguide.org.uk

Commission for Social Care Inspection (England)
33 Greycoat Street
London SW1P 2QF
Helplines: 0845 015 0120/0191 233 3323 (8.30 a.m. to 5.30 p.m., Monday to Friday)
Website: www.csci.org.uk

The Compassionate Friends
53 North Street
Bristol BS3 1EN
Helpline: 0845 123 2304 (10 a.m. to 4 p.m./6.30 p.m. to 10.30 p.m. every day)
Website: www.tcf.org.uk

Contact a Family
209–211 City Road
London EC1V 1JN
Tel.: 020 7608 8700
Helpline: 0808 808 3555
Website: www.cafamily.org.uk

The Continence Foundation
307 Hatton Square
16 Baldwins Gardens
London EC1N 7RJ
Helpline: 0845 345 0165 (9.30 a.m. to 1 p.m., Monday to Friday)
Website: www.continence-foundation.org.uk

Cruse Bereavement Care
PO Box 800
Richmond
Surrey TW9 1RG
Tel.: 020 8939 9530
Helpline: 0844 477 9400
Website: www.crusebereavementcare.org.uk
Youth website: www.rd4u.org.uk

Department for Transport/UK Disabled Persons Transport Advisory Committee (DPTAC)
Zone 4/24, Great Minster House
76 Marsham Street
London SW1P 4DR
Tel.: 020 7944 8011/Textphone 020 7944 3277
Website: www.dptac.gov.uk

Department of Health
Richmond House
79 Whitehall
London SW1A 2NS
Tel.: 020 7210 4850
Website: www.dh.gov.uk

Department of Work and Pensions
Disability Benefit Centre
3 Olympic House
Olympic Way
Wembley HA9 0DL
Tel.: 020 8795 8400
Website: www.dwp.gov.uk
Jobcentre Plus website: www.jobcentreplus.gov.uk
The Pension Service website: www.thepensionservice.gov.uk

DIAL UK
St Catherine's
Tickhill Road
Doncaster
South Yorkshire DN4 8QN
Tel.: 01302 310 123
Website: www.dialuk.info/

The Directory of Social Change
24 Stephenson Way
London NW1 2DP
Tel.: 020 7391 4800
Helpline: 08450 77 77 07
Website: www.dsc.org.uk

Aims to be an internationally
recognized independent source of
information and support to voluntary
and community sectors worldwide.

The Disability Law Service
Ground Floor
39–45 Cavell Street
London E1 2BP
Tel.: 020 7791 9800
Website: www.dls.org.uk

The Disability Rights Commission
Freepost MID02164
Stratford upon Avon CV37 9BR
Helpline: 08457 622 633
Website: www.drc-gb.org

Disabled Living Foundation
380–384 Harrow Road
LondonW9 2HU
Tel.: 020 7289 6111
Helpline: 0845 130 9177 (10 a.m. to 4
p.m., Monday to Friday)
Website: www.dlf.org.uk

Every Disabled Child Matters
c/o Council for Disabled Children
8 Wakley Street
London EC1V 7QE
Tel.: 020 7843 6448
Website: www.edcm.org.uk

**The Expert Patient Programme
Community Interest Company**
Tel.: 020 8249 6464
Website: www.expertpatients.nhs.uk
Email: admin.centralsupport@nhsepp.
org

The Eye Care Trust
PO Box 804
Aylesbury
Buckinghamshire HP20 9DF
Tel.: 0845 129 5001
Website: www.eyecaretrust.org.uk

The Family Fund
Unit 4, Alpha Court
Monks Cross Drive
Huntington
York YO32 9WN
Tel.: 0845 130 4542
Website: www.familyfund.org.uk

Forum of Mobility Centres
National Enquiry Line: 0800 559
3636
Website: www.mobility-centres.org.uk

Golden Lane Housing
West Point
Ground Floor
501 Chester Road
Old Trafford
Manchester M16 9HU
Tel.: 0845 604 0046
Website: www.glh.org.uk

Help the Hospices
Hospice House
34–44 Britannia Street
London WC1X 9JG
Tel.: 020 7520 8200
Website: www.helpthehospices.org.uk
Another useful website is: www.
hospiceinformation.info/

HM Revenue and Customs

For taxes and tax credits (anything
formerly dealt with by the Inland
Revenue) – contact your local enquiry
centre. The address should be in the
local phone book or you can find it
on the HM Revenue and Customs
website.
For general enquiries on customs,
excise, VAT and any other duties
formerly dealt with by HM Customs
and Excise
Tel.: 0845 010 9000 (8 a.m. to 8 p.m.
Monday to Friday)
Website: www.hmrc.gov.uk

Holiday Care see Tourism for All

Independent Practice: College of Occupational Therapists Specialist Section
Tel.: 0800 389 4873
Website: www.otip.co.uk

John Grooms
50 Scrutton Street
London EC2A 4XQ
Tel.: 020 7452 2000
Website: www.johngrooms.org.uk

Leonard Cheshire
30 Millbank
London SW1P 4QD
Tel.: 020 7802 8200
Website: www.Leonard-cheshire.org

Mobilise
Ashwellthorpe
Norwich NR16 1EX
Tel.: 01508 489449
Website: www.justwebs.
co.uk/mobilise

Motability
City Gate House
22 Southwark Bridge Road
London SE1 9HB
Tel.: 0845 456 4566
Website: www.motability.co.uk

The National Association of Bereavement Services
Second Floor
4 Pinchin Street
London E1 6DB
Helpline: 020 7709 9090, 10 a.m. to 4 p.m. weekdays

The National Council for Voluntary Organizations
Regent's Wharf
9 All Saints Street
London N1 9RL
Tel.: 020 7713 6161
Website: www.ncvo-vol.org.uk

National Debtline
Tricorn House
51–53 Hagley Road
Edgbaston
Birmingham B16 8TP
Freephone: 0808 808 4000
Website: www.nationaldebtline.org.uk

National Pharmacy Association
Mallison House
38–42 St Peter's Street
St Albans
Herts AL1 3NP
Tel.: 01727 832161
Patient website: www.
askyourpharmacist.co.uk

NHS Direct (England and Northern Ireland)
Tel.: 0845 46 47
Minicom: 0845 606 4647
Website: www.nhs.direct.nhs.uk

NHS Direct Wales
Tel.: 0845 46 47
Website: www.nhsdirect.wales.nhs.uk

NHS24 (Scotland)
Tel.: 08454 24 24 24
Website: www.nhs24.co.uk

The Northern Ireland Association for Mental Health
Central Office
80 University Street
Belfast BT7 1HE
Tel.: 028 9032 8474
Website: www.niamh.co.uk

Occupational Benevolent Funds Alliance (OBFA)
See **Association of Charity Officers**

Occupational Therapists in Independent Practice
See **Independent Practice**

One Parent Families
255 Kentish Town Road
London NW5 2LX
Tel.: 020 7428 5400
Helpline: 0800 018 5026
Website: www.oneparentfamilies.org.
uk

Patient Advice and Liaison Services
Contact your local primary care trust.

The Patients Association
PO Box 935
Harrow
Middlesex HA1 3YJ
Helpline: 08456 084455
Website: www.patients-association.
org.uk

The Pension Service
Tel.: 0845 60 60 265
Website: www.thepensionservice
.gov.uk

Primary Care Trusts
In your local phone directory or via
the following websites:

England: www.nhs.uk
Northern Ireland: www.
healthandcareni.co.uk
Scotland: www.show.scot.nhs.uk
(organizational information)
Wales: www.wales.nhs.uk

Public Guardianship Office
Archway Tower
2 Junction Road
London N19 5SZ
Tel.: 0845 330 2900
Website: www.guardianship.gov.uk

**Regulation and Quality
Improvement Authority (Northern
Ireland)**
9th Floor, Riverside Tower
5 Lanyon Place
Belfast BT1 3BT
Tel.: 028 9051 7500
Website: www.rqia.org.uk

Monitors and regulates the quality
of health and social-care services in
Northern Ireland.

Relate
Herbert Gray College
Little Church Street
Rugby
Warwickshire CV21 3AP
Tel.: 0845 456 1310
Website: www.relate.org.uk

**The Relatives and Residents
Association**
24 The Ivories
6–18 Northampton Street
London N1 2HY
Helpline: 020 7359 8136 (9.30 a.m. to
4.30 p.m., Monday to Friday)
Website: www.relres.org

Ricability
30 Angel Gate
City Road
London EC1V 2PT
Tel.: 020 7427 2460
Website: www.ricability.org.uk

The trading name for the Research
Institute for Consumer Affairs, a
charity that publishes consumer
information for people with
disabilities and elderly people.

**The Royal Association for
Disability and Rehabilitation
(RADAR)**
12 City Forum
250 City Road
London EC1V 8AF
Tel.: 020 7250 3222
Website: www.radar.org.uk

Royal College of Psychiatrists
17 Belgrave Square
London SW1X 8PG
Tel: 020 7235 2351
Website: www.rcpsych.ac.uk

**The Royal College of Speech and
Language Therapists**
2 White Hart Yard
London SE1 1NX
Tel.: 020 7378 1200
Website: www.rcslt.org.uk

**The Royal Pharmaceutical Society
of Great Britain**
1 Lambeth High Street
London SE1 7JN
Tel.: 020 7735 9141
Website: www.rpsgb.org.uk

SAGA
The Saga Building
Middelburg Square
Folkestone
Kent CT20 1AZ
Tel.: 0800 414 525
Website: www.saga.co.uk

Samaritans
Chris, PO Box 9090
Stirling FK8 2SA
Tel.: 08457 90 90 90
Website: www.samaritans.org.uk

The Scottish Association for Mental Health
Cumbrae House
15 Carlton Court
Glasgow G5 9JP
Tel.: 0141 568 7000
Website: www.samh.org.uk

The Scottish Commission for the Regulation of Care
Compass House
11 Riverside Drive
Dundee DD1 4NY
Tel: 01382 207100
Website: www.carecommission.com

Shared Care Network
Units 63–66, Easton Business Centre
Felix Road
Bristol BS5 OHE
Tel.: 0117 941 5361
Website: www.sharedcarenetwork.org.uk

The Society of Chiropodists and Podiatrists
1 Fellmonger's Path
Tower Bridge Road
London SE1 3LY
Tel.: 020 7234 8620
Website: www.feetforlife.org

Sue Ryder Care
Second Floor
114–118 Southampton Row
London WC1B 5AA
Tel.: 020 7400 0440
Website: www.sueryardercare.org.uk

Thrive
Sir Geoffrey Udall Centre
Beech Hill
Reading RG7 2AT
Tel: 0118 988 5688
Blind Gardeners' Helpline: 0118 988 6668
Website: www.thrive.org.uk

Aims to enable positive change in the lives of disabled and disadvantaged people through the use of gardening.

Tourism for All UK (formerly Holiday Care)
c/o Vitalise
Shap Road Industrial Estate
Kendal
Cumbria LA9 6NZ
Tel.: 0845 124 9971 (information)
0845 124973 (reservations)
Website: www.tourismforall.org.uk

UK Home Care Association
Group House
2nd Floor, 52 Sutton Court Road
Sutton
Surrey SM1 4SL
Tel.: 020 8288 5291
Website: www.ukhca.co.uk

Vitalise
Shap Road Industrial Estate
Kendal
Cumbria LA9 6NZ
Tel: 0845 330 0149
Website: www.vitalise.org.uk

Whizz-Kidz
Elliot House
10–12 Allington Street
London SW1E 5EH
Tel.: 020 7233 6600

Winston's Wish
The Clara Burgess Centre
Bayshill Road
Cheltenham GL50 3AW
Tel.: 01242 515157
Helpline: 08452 03 04 05
Website: www.winstonswish.org.uk

Working Families
1–3 Berry Street
London EC1V 0AA
Te.: 020 7253 7243
Website: www.workingfamilies.org.uk

Notes

1   Ten facts about caring. Carers UK website <www.carersuk.org> (accessed August 2005).
2   Can be viewed at <www.opsi.gov.uk/acts/acts1995/Ukpga_19950012_en_1.htm> (accessed June 2006).
3   Can be viewed at <www.opsi.gov.uk/acts/acts2000/20000016.htm> (accessed June 2006).
4   Can be viewed at <www.opsi.gov.uk/ACTS/acts2004/20040015.htm> (accessed June 2006).
5   Department of Health. Caring about carers: A national strategy for carers, 1999. Available at <www.dh.gov.uk> (accessed August 2005).
6   www.carers.gov.uk
7   Carers UK policy briefing 1998, Black and Minority Ethnic Carers <www.carersuk.org/Policyandpractice/PolicyResources/Policybriefings>
8   www.devon.gov.uk/index/socialcare/carers/caring-for-someone/bme-carers.htm
9   Carers UK policy briefing 2003, Lesbian and Gay Carers <www.carersuk.org/Policyandpractice/PolicyResources/Policybriefings>
10 Taken from information on rare disorders published by Contact a Family <www.cafamily.org.uk>
11 www.dh.gov.uk
12 Based on information in the NHS careers website, <www.nhscareers.nhs.uk>
13 Based on information on the NHS careers website, <www.nhscareers.nhs.uk> and the British Society for Oral Health and Disability website, <www.bsdh.org.uk>
14 www.carersuk.org (Carers UK)
15 www.carersuk.org (Carers UK)
16 Taken from information on the Carers UK website <www.carersuk.org>
17 www.dh.gov.uk
18 *Debt and Disability*, The Joseph Rowntree Foundation, 1995. See <www.jrf.org.uk/knowledge/findings/socialpolicy/SP78.asp>
19 *Debt and Disability: The impact of debt on families with disabled children*, Contact a Family and The Family Fund, 2004. See <www.cafamily.org.uk/debtsummary.pdf>
20 Sandra Haurant, 'Citizens Advice reports upsurge in serious debt', *The Guardian*, 7 November 2006 <www.guardian.co.uk>
21 Action for carers and employment website <www.acecarers.org.uk>
22 Carers UK, *Juggling Work and Care*, Carers UK, 2005 <www.carersuk.org/Employers>
23 www.mssociety.org.uk
24 Hugh Marriott, *The Selfish Pig's Guide to Caring*, Polperro Heritage

Press, 2003, p. 18. Extracts in this chapter are used with permission of Polperro Heritage Press.

25 Available from <www.parkinsons.org.uk>

26 Toni Battison, *Caring for Someone with Memory Loss*, Age Concern Books, 2004.

27 Princess Royal Trust for Carers website <www.carers.org>

28 Be prepared: A carers guide to planning for emergencies <www.carersuk. org.uk>

29 Some of this is based on *International Travel and Parkinson's*, Parkinson's Disease Society, May 2006.

30 www.teachernet.gov.uk

31 www.direct.gov.uk

32 See <www.cafamily.org.uk/packs.html>

33 See <www.cafamily.org.uk/eduscot.html>

34 Figures and statements for this paragraph from Contact a Family <www. cafamily.org.uk>

35 www.carers.org

36 www.direct.gov.uk

37 Carers UK, *Juggling Work and Care*, <www.carersuk.org>

38 Doris Stickney, *Waterbugs and Dragonflies*, London, Continuum International Publishing Group Ltd., 2002.

39 Partly based on Bridget McCall, 'Information for Partners, Families and friends', in *Parkinson's Disease Self-Care Manual*, The September Foundation, Amsterdam, 2000.

Further reading

Barbara Baker (2003), *When Someone You Love has Depression*, London, Sheldon Press.

Frankie Campling and Michael Sharpe (2006), *Living with a Long-term Illness: The facts*, Oxford, Oxford University Press.

Lorna Easterbrook (2005), *Your Rights to Health Care*, London, Age Concern Books.

Mary V. Goudge (2004), *Choosing a Care Home*, Oxford, How to Books.

Helen Howard (2004), *Caring for Someone in Their Own Home*, London, Age Concern Books.

Deborah Hutton (2005), *What Can I Do to Help?*, London, Short Books.

Jacqui Jackson (2004), *Multicoloured Mayhem: Parenting the many shades of adolescents and children with autism, asperger syndrome and AD/HD*, London, Jessica Kingsley Publishers.

Luke Jackson (2002), *Freaks, Geeks and Asperger Syndrome*, London, Jessica Kingsley Publishers.

Audrey Jenkinson (2004), *Past Caring*, Clifton-on-Teme, Worcestershire, Polperro Heritage Press.

Mary Jordan (2006), *The Essential Carer's Guide*, London, Hammersmith Press Ltd.

Abigail Knight (2002), *Caring for a Disabled Child* (third edition), London, Straightforward Press Ltd.

Marina Lewycka (2003), *Carers Handbook: What to do and who to turn to*, London, Age Concern Books.

Penny Mares (2003), *Caring for Someone Who is Dying*, London, Age Concern Books.

Hugh Marriott (2003), *The Selfish Pig's Guide to Caring*, Clifton-on-Teme, Worcestershire, Polperro Heritage Press.

Julia Phillips, Miriam Bernard and Minda Chittenden (2002), *Juggling Work and Care: The experiences of working carers of older adults*, London, Policy Press.

Rachel Naomi Remen (1997), *Kitchen Table Wisdom*, London, Pan Books.

Marian Shoard (2004), *A Survival Guide to Later Life*, London, Constable and Robinson Ltd.

Bernie Siegel (1999), *Love, Medicine and Miracles*, London, Rider and Co.

Tom Smith (2007), *How to Get the Best from Your Doctor*, London, Sheldon Press.

Julie Spencer-Cingöz (2003), *Caring for Someone at a Distance*, London, Age Concern Books.

Rosie Staal (2006), *What Shall We Do with Mother?*, Great Ambrook, Devon, White Ladder Press Ltd.

John Stanford (ed.) (2007), *If Only I'd Known That a Year Ago: A guide for newly disabled people, their families and friends*, London, Royal Association for Disability and Rehabilitation.

Index

Abbeyfield 95
accidents 35
Action for Carers and Employment (ACE) 9, 47–8
Action on Elder Abuse 13
Adults with Incapacity 44
Age Concern 12, 13
  advice about payments 33
  carers' handbooks 15
  Caring for Someone at a Distance 80
  community alarms 35, 64
  financial advice 43
  Your Rights to Health Care (Easterbrook) 27
alarm systems 35
Alzheimer Scotland – Action on Dementia 13
Alzheimer's Society 13
Anchor Trust 95
Arthritis Care 13, 62
Association for Spina Bifida and Hydrocephalus (ASBAH) 74
Association of Children's Hospices 97

Bandolier (journal/website) 15
Barnardo's 13, 74
  young carers 90
bereavement 96
  young carers 89
Blue Badge scheme 37
Brain & Spine Foundation 13
Brewin, Rena 10–11
British Broadcasting Corporation (BBC) 16
British Heart Foundation 13
British Medical Association 15

cancer organizations 12
Cancerbackup 12
Care and Repair 36
CareAware 34
carers
  Allowances 42
  creative outlets 53–4
  defining 1–2, 86
  at a distance 79–85
  keeping a diary 101
  looking after yourself 58
  needs of 2
  organizations for 3–4
  paying for care 32–3
  personal impact on 52–60
  recognition for 2–4
  self-management strategies 101
  statistics of 86
  stopping caring 94–5
Carers and Children Act (2000) 3
Carers and Disabled Children Act (2000) 9, 29
carer's assessments 5, 29–32, 56, 100
  paying for care 32–3
Carers (Equal Opportunities) Act (2004) 3, 47
Carers' Opportunities Fund 51
Carers (Recognition and Services) Act (1995) 3, 9
  assessments and 29
Carers UK 9–10, 12
  assessments and 30, 31
  financial advice 43
  'Juggling and Work' 49
  'Looking After Someone' 33
  statistics of carers 1
CarersLine 9
Caring for a Disabled Child (Knight) 75
Caring for Someone at a Distance (Spencer-Cingöz) 80
Caring (magazine) 9
Centre for Accessible Environments 36
Charity Choice/Charities Digest 13
Charity Search 43
Cheshire, Leonard *see* Leonard Cheshire
Childline 87, 90
children 73–8
  adolescence 73
  as carers 86–93
  diagnosis 69–70
  disability benefits 41–2
  education 71
  finances 72
  parent carers 70
  services for 70
  statistics of 69
  surviving parents 73
Children Act (1989) 70
Children's Society 13, 74, 90
  Young Carers Initiative 88, 90
Choosing a Care Home (Goudge) 95–6
Citizens Advice 11, 13–14
  advice about payments 33
  after a death 96
  financial advice 43, 44
City and Guilds
  Learning for Living 50

CLIC Sargent 74
Commission for Social Care Inspection 34, 95
community alarm systems 35, 64, 84
community care 29–32
Community Care Act 70
Compassionate Friends 97
Complete Care Home Guide (Counsel and Care) 95–6
computers 35–6, 81
    online services 83
Contact a Family 13, 14, 40, 42, 53, 69, 98
    advocates 77
    'Benefits, Tax Credits and Other Financial Help' 72
    Directory of Specific Conditions, Rare Disorders 74
    disabled children 73–4
    Disabled Education and Disability 71
    Post 16 Transition 73
    Transition: England and Wales 73
continence advisors 25–6
Counsel and Care 13
    advice about payments 33
    Complete Care Home Guide 95
counselling 26–7
creative outlets 53–4
Cri du Chat syndrome 77
Crossroads – Caring for Carers 63, 67–8
    young carers 90, 92–3
Cruse 89, 97

Darke, May 92–3
dental care 20
depression 13, 56
Depression Alliance 13
Diabetes UK 13
diet and nutrition 23
Directory of Social Change 42–3
disability
    see illness and disability
Disability Discrimination Act
    protection of 39
    public transport and 38
Disability Information and Advice Line 4
Disability Living Allowance 32
Disability Rights Commission 39
Disabled Living Foundation 35, 36
    'Sources of Funding and Obtaining Equipment' 42
Disabled Persons Transport Advisory Committee 39
Down's Syndrome Association 13
driving 36–7

Easterbrook, Lorna
    Your Rights to Health Care 27
education
    for carers 2, 47, 49–51
    computers and 36
    disabled children 71
    for disabled people 4
    young carers and 88
emergencies
    community alarm systems 35, 64, 84
    at a distance 79–80
    planning for 64–5
emotional and psychological impacts 101
    bereavement 96–9
    depression and burnout 56
    of diagnosis 69–70
    impact on carers 52–3
    respite care and 63–4
    young carers 87–93
employment
    ACE 11
    after a death 97–8, 99
    'Back to Work' courses 11
    for carers 47–9
equipment 34–5, 35
ethnicity and race 11–12
Eurodis 14
Every Child Matters 75
everyday activities 1, 6
    adaptations to the home 36
Expert Patient Programme
    Community Interest Company 49–50, 101
Eye Care Trust 21

Fair Deal Campaign 10
The Family Fund 40, 42
financial matters 40–1, 101
    after a death 96, 97
    benefits 104
    children 72
    debt 43–4
    Disability Living Allowance 76
    non-governmental support 42–3
    power of attorney 44
    respite care 63
    struggling with 1
    welfare benefits 41–2
Forum of Mobility Centres 39
Foundation for People with Learning Difficulties 12–13
Freaks, Geeks and Asperger Syndrome (Jackson) 78

gay and lesbian carers 12
generalized torsion dystonia 4
Golden Lane Housing 95
Goudge, Mary V.
 Choosing a Care Home 95–6
Grooms (John) services 95
guilt feelings 6

healthcare professionals 5, 101–2
 dentists 20
 at a distance 80, 81–2
 doctors 19
 giving a diagnosis 55–6
 information from 7, 8
 NHS Direct 17
 nurses 19–20
 opticians 21
 pharmacists 24–5
 talking to 27–8
 therapists 21–4
 see also National Health Service
Help the Aged 13
 community alarms 35, 64
Help the Hospices 13, 89, 97
hospitals, day 26

illness and disability
 children 69–70
 diagnosis of 55–6, 69–70
 Disability Living Allowance 76
 public toilets 38
 rare disorders 14, 74
 welfare benefits 41–2
information 2, 8, 100–1
 about conditions 6
 government sources 3
 media and medicine 14–15
 from organizations 9–14

Jackson, Jacqui
 Multicoloured Mayhem 78
Jackson, Luke
 Freaks, Geeks and Asperger Syndrome
 78
Jenkinson, Audrey
 Past Caring: The beginning not the end
 99
Jobcentre Plus 49, 97–8

Knight, Abigail
 Caring for a Disabled Child 75

Learndirect 50–1
learning disabilities 12–13
legal matters

power of attorney 44
 wills 45, 96
Leonard Cheshire services 95
libraries 16
local authorities 30
Looking After Me 50
Loughborough University 89

Macmillan Cancer Support 12
Marriott, Hugh 53–4
 The Selfish Pig's Guide to Caring 55,
 59–60
MDF The BiPolar Organisation 13
medications
 pharmacists 24–5
 for rare disorders 14
 travelling with 65–6
men and women carers 1
Mencap 12, 53, 74
 respite care and holidays 62
Mental Health Foundation 13
Mind 13
 Making Sense of Counselling 27
Misuse of Drugs Act 65–6
Mobilise 39
Motor Neurone Association 13
Multicoloured Mayhem (Jackson) 78
Multiple Sclerosis (MS) Society 13, 51,
 . 90–1

National Association of Bereavement
 Services 97
National Autistic Society 13, 74
National Council for Voluntary
 Organizations 13
National Deaf Children's Society 74
National Extension College 51
National Health Service
 hospital care 18–19
 NHS Direct 17
 primary care 17–18
NCH, the children's charity 13, 74, 90
Northern Ireland Association for Mental
 Health 13

occupational therapy 22–3, 36
 equipment 34
One Parent Families 74
opticians 21
Orphanet 14

Parents and Paediatricians Together
 98
parking badges 37
Parkinson's disease 5–6

Parkinson's Disease Society 13, 16
  assessment help 31
  Holidays and Respite Care Guide 61
Past Caring: The beginning not the end
  (Jenkinson) 99
Patient Advice and Liaison Services
  (PALS) 18
Patient UK 13
Patients Association 27
pensions 42
physiotherapy 21–2, 34
podiatry/chiropody 23–4
Princess Royal Trust for Carers 4, 10–11,
  12
  after a death 96
  assessment 33
  bursaries for carers 50, 51
  financial advice 43
  respite information 61
  young carers 86, 87, 89–90
psychiatry 26, 57
psychologists 26–7
Public Guardianship Office 44

Quackwatch 15

Rachel House 92, 99
rehabilitation centres 26
relationships
  of carers 54–5
  families with disabled children 72
  feeling isolated 1, 4
  sexual 54–5
  social life of young carers 88
Relatives and Residents Association 95
religion 57–8
residential care 94–5
respite care and holidays 2, 61–2, 66–8,
  104
  emergencies and 64–5
  financing 63
  at home 62–3
  need for 63–4
  travelling abroad 65–6
Rethink 13
Ricability 39
Rowntree (Joseph) Foundation 40
Royal Association for Disability and
  Rehabilitation 13, 34, 38
Royal College of Paediatrics and Child
  Health 98
Royal College of Psychiatrists 97
  'Spirituality and Mental Health' 57
Royal National Institute for the Blind 74

Ryder, Sue *see* Sue Ryder

Samaritans 13
Sane 13
Scope 74
Scottish Association for Mental Health
  13
The Selfish Pig's Guide to Caring
  (Marriott) 55, 59–60
Shared Care Network 62
Sheldon Press 16
Smith, Dr Tom
  How to Get the Best from Your Doctor 27
Social Care Institute for Excellence 49
social services 5, 101–2
  asking questions of 7
  assessments and 30, 32
  at a distance 81
  paying for care 32–3
  social workers 25
speech and language therapy 22, 34
Spencer-Cingöz, Julie
  Caring for Someone at a Distance 80
spirituality 57–8
Stanford, John
  If Only I'd Known That a Year Ago 34
Stroke Association 13
Sue Ryder organization 95
support and support groups 2, 7, 52–3
  family 6
  information from 16
  young carers 89–91
Supporting Parents Programme 50

toilets, public 38
Tourism for All 62
transport
  driving and parking 36–7
  public 38

UK Home Care Association 63
United Kingdom
  Caring About Carers 3
  website information 3

Vitalise 62

Whizz-Kidz 75
Williams, Liz 28
Winston's Wish 89, 97
Work and Families Act 47
Working Families 48

Young Minds 90